W9-CBG-689

A RUSH
TO
INJUSTICE

HOW POWER, PREJUDICE, RACISM, AND POLITICAL CORRECTNESS
OVERSHADOWED TRUTH AND JUSTICE IN THE
DUKE LACROSSE RAPE CASE

A RUSH
TO
INJUSTICE

HOW POWER, PREJUDICE, RACISM, AND POLITICAL CORRECTNESS OVERSHADOWED TRUTH AND JUSTICE IN THE DUKE LACROSSE RAPE CASE

NADER BAYDOUN
AND
R. STEPHANIE GOOD

THOMAS NELSON
Since 1798

NASHVILLE   DALLAS   MEXICO CITY   RIO DE JANEIRO   BEIJING

Published in Nashville, TN, by Thomas Nelson. Thomas Nelson is a trademark of Thomas Nelson, Inc.

Published in association with the literary agency of Wolgemuth & Associates.

Thomas Nelson, Inc. titles may be purchased in bulk for educational, business, fundraising, or sales promotional use. For information, please e-mail SpecialMarkets@thomasnelson.com.

Library of Congress Cataloging-in-Publication data
on file with the Library of Congress.

ISBN 10: 1-59555-118-2
ISBN 13: 978-1-59555-118-4

Printed in the United States of America

07 08 09 10 11 QW 5 4 3 2 1

CONTENTS

This book is dedicated to David Evans, Collin Finnerty, Reade Seligmann, all of the members of the Duke University Men's Lacrosse Team, and their families, all of whom have suffered so much at the hands of those who lost sight of the true meaning of justice, honesty, and human decency. I hope that this book portrays their story accurately and fairly and that it helps to exonerate the three young men who were wrongfully accused, and to obliterate any notions of guilt of any member of the Duke University Men's Lacrosse Team. May these young men and their families be able to walk through the rest of their lives knowing that the outrageous lies that have been perpetrated against them have been exposed, that they have now finally been completely exonerated by the legal system, and that the truth will be known by anyone who is fair-minded enough to simply look at the facts that have been presented herein.

ACKNOWLEDGMENTS

There are numerous people to thank for helping to make this book possible, all of whom have my sincerest and deepest gratitude.

I would like to begin by thanking my wonderful wife, Barbara, for her constant love, encouragement, and support, and for allowing me to take the time to bring this important story to the forefront in order to expose a terrible injustice while presenting the truth.

I would like to thank my friend, R. Stephanie Good, whose excellent research and writing skills and experience were invaluable in helping me put this book together.

I would also like to thank my good friend, Durham attorney Wes Covington, who was the first person to help put the facts and the parties involved with the lacrosse case into the proper perspective for me, and for directing me to other valuable sources of information to uncover the truth.

I am especially grateful to Durham attorney, Bob Ekstrand, and his paralegal, Stefanie Sparks, whose dedication to seeking justice for Evans, Finnerty, and Seligmann and their teammates contributed so much to their defense as well as to this book. Their tireless efforts in assisting us by providing us with valuable information and leads for sources of information were crucial to compiling the facts for this book. I am very thankful to both of them for their gracious contributions to this project.

I also extend my appreciation to Durham attorney, Bill Thomas, for taking the time to meet with us and offer so much valuable information for this book.

I would like to thank Durham attorney Eddie Falcone for taking the time to meet with me and provide me with information for this book.

I would also like to thank and acknowledge Duke Law School Professors James E. Coleman, Jr. and Paul Haagan, and Duke Chemistry Professor Dr. Steven Baldwin for taking the time to meet with us, and especially for having the courage to speak out on behalf of the lacrosse team and for contributing so much essential information to this book.

A heartfelt thank you to Reade Seligmann's attorney, the late J. Kirk Osborn, whose insight in allowing his defense motions to be published on the Internet for all to see helped to open the eyes of so many. Having access to these well-written motions enabled us to include an abundance of essential and informative material in this book.

I also want to give warm and special thanks to my close friend and agent, Robert Wolgemuth, whose counsel, friendship, and support have been invaluable to me.

A special thank you to the wonderful people at Thomas Nelson Publishing, especially David Dunham and Joel Miller, for allowing me the opportunity to tell this important story, and to my editor, Alice Sullivan, for working so hard to make this book a reality.

I want to thank my good friend and fellow Dukie, Larry "Satch" Saunders, for allowing me to share my thoughts and ideas with him while compiling this book.

ACKNOWLEDGMENTS

To the Duke University students who came forward to offer their opinions and information, I thank you. May you never experience the injustice that has been inflicted upon your classmates.

May God bless and keep each and every one of you.

1

THE
BEGINNING

By now you probably know the truth: First, a stripper who was hired to dance at a party thrown by members of the Duke University lacrosse team claimed that she was brutally gang raped, sodomized, and beaten. Then the situation took on a life of its own and spun out of control. The horrific allegations of gang rape became entwined with the outrageous lies of a rogue prosecutor who took down everyone around him, including several individuals, a university, a town, and ultimately, himself.

It began on Monday night, March 13, 2006, when about forty young men were crammed into a tiny rented house at 610 North Buchanan Boulevard. Mostly members of the Duke University lacrosse team, they could not participate in the usual spring break festivities because of conflicts with their practice schedule. They had to celebrate by other means. A blowout party had become something of a tradition. But this year, the entertainment would leave team members with a night they would never forget.

The first stripper, a thirty-one-year-old African American woman named Kim Pittman, a.k.a. Kim Roberts, showed up at about 11:15 that night. Roughly half an hour later, the second stripper, twenty-seven-year-old Crystal Gail Mangum, an African American mother of two, was dropped off by her boyfriend. According to Mangum's handwritten statement, given to authorities more than three weeks later, when she arrived at the party Roberts was already "in the backyard" surrounded by "about ten guys, and they were all holding drinks."

3

According to Mangum, she and Roberts introduced themselves to each other and "talked for about five minutes." They didn't know each other but were there for the same reason—fast cash for an easy gig.

With pleasantries exchanged, both women entered through the rear door of the house, accompanied by several of the partygoers. Roberts, who danced under the name "Nikki," went to the bathroom and changed into her costume. Mangum, who used the name "Precious," arrived dressed to dance but followed Nikki inside to continue talking. While Nikki prepared herself, one of the guys knocked on the door and offered them drinks. They accepted and kept talking, but as far as the boys were concerned, talking wasn't on the night's agenda. They grew impatient.

"What's the problem?" two guys asked through the door. Mangum said that they tried pushing their way inside, insisting, "Get out here and dance." Soon there were more than a dozen boys at the door shouting, "Come on. Show us something. Let's see some action." Temporarily stilling the boys' mounting frustration, Nikki and Precious emerged just before midnight.

Surrounded by the boys, Nikki and Precious began their routine—but something wasn't right. First, there was all the impatience and yelling. Now, while some of the lacrosse players snapped pictures of the dancing girls, most of them sat around disinterested in the show. Then Mangum said she heard it.

"Let's f— these black bitches. We are going to f— you black bitches." This was no easy gig. It was getting dangerous.

According to Mangum, she and Nikki began to cry. Mangum decided to get dressed, get her money, and leave. According to her April 6, 2006, statement, the two women ran "screaming and crying" out to the car. Two of the partiers followed them outside and "apologized to Nikki," allegedly offering the women $12,000 to come back in and continue dancing. Mangum claimed that she and Nikki went back

4

into the house, but once inside realized that things were worse than before. The boys "were more excited and angry," she said, and screamed, "We are going to f— you black bitches. We are going to stick broomsticks up your ass."

Mangum alleged that she and Nikki tried to leave again, but "three guys grabbed Nikki, and 'Brett,' 'Adam,' and 'Matt'" separated the two women while they tried to hang on to each other. Mangum said that "Brett, Adam, and Matt" pulled her into the bathroom while the other guys sat close by in the living room watching television.

"Sweetheart, you can't leave," Matt told her, according to Mangum, but her nightmare was only beginning. The three guys allegedly raped and sexually assaulted her "anally, vaginally, and orally" while yelling racial slurs at her, during which time the men also allegedly "hit and kicked" her. She added that "Adam ejaculated in [her] mouth and [she] spit it out onto the bathroom floor."

As Mangum told it, they boys really worked her over. She said that after the alleged attack, Nikki and Adam dressed her and "dragged her out to [Roberts's] car" because her "legs wouldn't work." She claimed that she told Nikki she was hurt, and Nikki was going to get her some help and call the police.

According to witnesses, before Roberts pulled away, some of the guys expressed their disappointment that they had paid the women and felt ripped off. It touched off a brief but loud tête-à-tête.

"Screw you," Roberts shouted from her car, "we're out of here."

"We can't believe we paid you for nothing," one guy yelled.

"You limp dick white boys had to pay us to come here," Roberts responded.

"Thank your grandpa for my nice white cotton shirt," taunted another boy.

Roberts, starting to drive off, slammed on her breaks. "Oh s—, that's a hate crime," she belted, "I'm calling the police!"

At approximately 12:53 a.m. (now March 14), Roberts, while still sitting in front of 610 North Buchanan, dialed 911. The boys, already apprehensive because of the events of the last hour, scattered. As far as they were concerned, the night was over. It was, but the ordeal was just beginning.

Within months of the alleged incident, there were precious few Americans who couldn't relate the rough outline of the story as told by the dancers. It was national news—and not just national news but one of those megastories that settles into the news cycle like a permanent houseguest. Like many, I watched the unfolding story because of the way it was massaged by producers into a riveting daily news serial. I was fascinated by it, but as developments in the case pointed to conflicts that undermined the integrity of the story, I had to find out more—from the front lines.

I went back to Duke University for the sole purpose of uncovering the truth. I have called Durham, North Carolina, my home, and I consider the people here to be my extended family. Often when I talk about them, I preface my comments with this opening line, "I bleed blue," or "I have blue blood running through my veins." I am not a member of a royal family. I am a "Dukie," a Duke University alumnus, and our colors are white and royal blue, also known as "Duke Blue."

I owe a huge debt of gratitude to this great institution because as a young man, I was recruited to attend Duke and was offered an athletic scholarship to play football there. Duke offered me the opportunity to attend one the nation's best academic institutions and play college football at the Division I level. Add to that the unique charm of the campus setting, the relatively small size of the student body, and the geographical climate, and it was not difficult to choose Duke. Having been the youngest of ten children in an immigrant family and the son of a grocery store owner, I could not have possibly attended such an elite school as Duke without the financial assistance they

6

offered. My studies there allowed me to continue my education at Vanderbilt Law School and to pursue a career in law. For over thirty years, I have enjoyed a successful law practice and have tried many cases, the subject matter of which encompasses a broad variety. I have been blessed beyond anything I might have imagined while growing up in humble beginnings in Detroit, Michigan, and having the opportunity to attend Duke has played a highly essential part of that. So, for many reasons, I am deeply indebted to Duke. As only the second person in my family to have graduated from high school at the time, I know what the alternatives could have been.

At Duke, I received a great education in the classroom. Equally important was the education that I received from spending time with my many classmates. I developed many close relationships with bright and talented people and learned a great deal because they all came from such diverse backgrounds compared to mine. Over the years, I have maintained many of those relationships and count many of them among my closest friends, mentors, and confidants. My daughter, Reagan, also attended Duke and graduated in 2001.

It is because of my love for and deep sense of loyalty to Duke that I came back here. I had to know the truth. But truth has been hard to come by. Due to the way the events of the past year have unfolded and been portrayed in the media, doubt came to overshadow the entire affair. But the doubt didn't thin the dark cloud that hovered over my school—the athletic department in particular—since March 2006. That cloud only began to lift more than a full year later.

There is one thing that I should make clear right from the outset: I did not come to Durham as an attorney. I came as a member of the Duke family. But in spite of my "blue-blooded" loyalty, my fidelity to Duke does not extend beyond the truth. I had no interest in covering up for the actions of any guilty party, and I would have done everything in my power to see that any crimes would not go unpunished.

When I first heard about the rape allegations, I was stunned. But the more I thought about it, the more implausible it seemed. The incident allegedly took place at a lacrosse team party where alcohol was served. Like many people at Duke, I attended college parties where drinking was involved. I was an athlete and a member of the Phi Delta Theta fraternity. I spent much of my time with other athletes, as well as many nonathletes. I also attended numerous parties thrown by athletes and fraternities. The one aspect of these rape allegations that did not make any sense to me was the notion that something this outrageous could occur in the midst of forty to fifty Duke students and no one had a strong enough sense of responsibility or the conscience to intervene and stop it. However, while it was hard to stomach the idea that a gang rape could have occurred in the midst of a large number of Duke students, I was determined to keep an open mind and see what the evidence revealed.

Although I had been following the case since shortly after the story broke in the news, my first trip back to Durham to investigate the incident was on February 5, 2007, and it took me to the office of an old friend, Wes Covington, another Duke alumnus. Wes is a well-respected attorney in Durham and someone who was involved in the case during the very early days of the investigation. I thought that if anyone could fill in the blanks for me, Wes could. But I had no idea just how many blanks there were until I sat down with him and the many others I interviewed.

As I listened to the stories, it became apparent that this case was never really about rape—not the rape of a young woman anyway. It had more to do with a gross abuse of power and one man's ability to totally distort justice and redefine it for his own purposes. The cast of characters that was being described to me thickened the plot so intensely that I began to wonder just how far the corruption in Durham truly reached. I heard tales of crooked prosecutors, selfserving faculty members, turncoat administrators, irate, revenge-seeking neighbors, and even, possibly, dirty cops who were out to pursue their own personal agendas. There was so much information that it was difficult to process it all, but I definitely wanted to learn the truth.

Wes first heard about the Duke rape allegations when he received a call from Sue Wasiolek a.k.a. "Dean Sue," the Assistant Vice President for Student Affairs and Dean of Students. Dean Wasiolek informed Wes that there was a problem with the lacrosse team, that there had been a party, and that allegations of sexual impropriety had been made.

According to the details that were related to me, the incident began during spring break of 2006, when three of the four captains of the nationally ranked Duke lacrosse team, Matt Zash, Dan Flannery, and David Evans, threw a party at their small, off-campus house. Throwing a party had become a ritual over the years because spring break usually occurred during the middle of the lacrosse season and the team had to remain on campus to practice. Since these team members could not take full advantage of spring break like the other students, they attended a party. As part of the evening's entertainment, Dan Flannery googled an escort service and hired two strippers to dance for the team. The players chipped in to cover the $800 fee that the women charged for their performance, which was to be for a two-hour period.

Several different versions of the events that transpired that evening have been offered, but the end result remained the same. A woman claimed that a rape occurred, and it turned the lives of countless people and an entire community upside down. Most significantly, it changed forever the lives of three Duke athletes and their families.

I continued my investigation and met with Bob Ekstrand, a Durham attorney who was an important player early in the case and the person who, along with his paralegal, Stefanie Sparks, put together a compelling timeline that confirmed the alibis of the boys (see Appendix). He offered his opinion about why Roberts probably called the police. He suggested that she just wanted to scare the boys. Apparently, having strippers is not that unusual at Duke. Bob said that the fraternities and sororities occasionally hire them. But the lacrosse team had never done this before. They were freaking out because their lacrosse coach, Mike Pressler, was a tough disciplinarian. Bob said, "He's a great person, in fact, one of the very few heroes in this case. He would run them until they puked if he found out about this." So when the night blew up in their faces, the boys were nervous, and wanted everybody out of there.

The boys were worried because of what had been going on with the authorities. According to Bob, in August 2005, the Durham police and the Alcohol Enforcement Agency hatched a plan to spend weekends rounding up as many kids as possible and charging them with misdemeanors—possession of alcohol and noise ordinance violations being the primary vehicles for charging them. One of the things they did was to find parties that appeared to be well attended by Duke students and began executing SWAT-style warrantless raids. Hundreds of kids were getting citations, and several of them were lacrosse players. It wasn't just happening in houses. Sometimes the kids would get pulled over for a no left turn signal violation and the police would yank them out of the car, perform a search and find an empty beer can, and charge all of the kids with possession of an open container in a vehicle. Then someone from the Dean of Students office would receive the police report and initiate a judicial affairs action against the kids and threaten to suspend them. This zealous crackdown created a real tension for the lacrosse players because Coach Pressler would find out and take disciplinary action.

Bob's theory was that Roberts was savvy enough to see that these kids were scared about the idea that the police might be coming. So she held her phone out and dialed 911 so the boys could see her call-ing. The way Roberts called in her complaint indicated that she really didn't want to cause too much trouble (the transcript of her call is available later in this chapter). It was just a scare tactic to get back at the boys for the verbal exchange that had taken place.

If Bob is right, Roberts opened up a Pandora's Box that night without even realizing it. And Mangum dumped out all of its con-tents. Obviously, Mangum's description of what allegedly happened to her on the night of March 13 was truly alarming.

On March 16, 2006, Mangum participated in a photo identifica-tion session where she was shown pictures to identify her alleged attackers. Investigators R.D. Clayton and Michelle Soucie of the Durham Police Department had four photo arrays that Mangum was going to view. Clayton did not compile the photos. Soucie partici-pated in that process after Durham Police Sgt. Mark Gottlieb and oth-ers had obtained pictures of the lacrosse team. Under Gottlieb's instructions, Soucie put only pictures of lacrosse team members into the four separate arrays so that each array would have photos of a potential "Matt," an "Adam," or a "Brett." Clayton and Soucie brought the arrays to Mangum's home "less than seventy-two hours after the alleged assault." The way the officers conducted the identification was to tell Mangum to "identify the 'person you saw [who] sexually assaulted you.'" The first photo array contained six pictures of Duke lacrosse team members, including that of Reade Seligmann. Mangum remarked that, "this was 'harder' than she thought it would be;" how-ever, she did pick Seligmann's photo, saying that she "was 70% sure she recognized [him]," but "could not remember where exactly she saw him at the party." She also "stated that the people in the photos looked alike." Mangum then claimed to "recognize with 100% cer-tainty" four other players in another array. However, one of the play-ers that she identified, Brad Ross, was out of town on the night of the party. At the end of viewing the fourth array, out of twenty-four pictures that Mangum looked at, she did not identify any of the people as her attackers.

On that same day, the three lacrosse team captains, Matt Zash, Dan Flannery, and David Evans, voluntarily aided police in executing a search warrant at their residence, 610 North Buchanan. They also voluntarily went to the police station to give statements and submit to DNA testing. While there, David Evans informed investigators that, besides those lacrosse players who were present at the party, there were "two or three fraternity guys" there and one of them "was named Blake." So the police were aware that non-lacrosse players had attended the party.

As soon as he heard about the incident, Bob Ekstrand began working hard to help the boys avoid any serious problems. He talked to some of the parents and offered legal assistance to the boys by either representing them or assisting them in retaining other attorneys.

Shortly thereafter, Dean Wasiolek contacted Wes and requested that he talk to the three lacrosse team captains to see what he could learn about the allegations. The following Saturday morning, March 18, 2006, Wes met with Zash, Flannery, and Evans for a couple of hours. Wes told me that he really put them through rigorous questioning in order to assure that their versions of the incident corresponded. He interviewed each captain individually while the other two were out of the room. Wes said that no matter what he tried to do, their stories were consistently solid, enabling him to come to the conclusion that no rape had taken place. Evidence that emerged as the case proceeded, Wes told me, was very much in line with what the guys had told him in their interviews that morning.

Wes also said that he went over to examine the residence where the party had been held. His description matched the pictures of the tiny white house at 610 North Buchanan Boulevard that had been splashed all over the news. He studied the premises, making it a point to see the bathroom where the woman claimed to have been raped by three men. He came to one very important conclusion: the bathroom is so small that it would be very difficult to fit four people in there at the same time, much less four people simultaneously engaged in violent sex. That description of the bathroom has been confirmed by several other sources.

On March 20, 2006, Kim Roberts was contacted by Investigator Benjamin Himan who questioned her about the night of the party. She was quoted in Himan's notes as saying that Mangum's rape allegations were a "crock." Two days later, Roberts gave a statement detailing the events of March 13 and 14, and it was very different from Mangum's.

According to the handwritten statement of "Kim Pittman Roberts," dated March 22, 2006, after Mangum arrived, the women were each offered a drink. Referring to Mangum as "Precious," Roberts said they started to dance, and it "seemed to be going well" until "Precious began showing signs of intoxication." While still putting on their show, things went downhill when "one of the boys brought out a broomstick" and offered to use it on the women. Roberts said that the comment "made her uncomfortable" so she announced that "the show is over." At that point, Roberts said, "the commotion got Precious riled up" and she became "irate." According to Roberts's statement, the women went into the bathroom. Roberts said that she wanted to leave, but Precious said they could "get more money." Precious became "uncontrollable" and began "yelling at the boys who were banging on the door." Roberts said that she took her things and went out to her car where she changed out of her costume and waited for Mangum.

Mangum came out, but said that she wanted to go back to make more money. Roberts said that after Mangum went back into the house, some of the guys came out to tell her that "Precious was passed out in the back," and they asked Roberts to do something. The guys then allegedly helped Mangum to the car. Although she didn't have the bag that she had arrived with, Mangum, seeming incoherent, insisted to Roberts that she did have the $400. But she wanted to go back inside because "there was more money to be made." Roberts, stating that she did not see Mangum's possessions, claimed she went back inside the house and Dan Flannery, one of the team's cocaptains, helped her look for them. She didn't find them, and she went back to the car to leave. At that point, she claimed, "the boys began yelling, 'Nigger,' at them." Roberts stated she called the police to report the racial slurs.

I had been reading that there were conflicting versions of the events of March 13, and I had heard different stories, but now I was reading the women's actual handwritten statements to the police. They didn't match up at all. Clearly, something was very wrong here.

Continuing my research, I came up with the audiotape of Roberts's 911 call.

I'm in Durham and I was driving down by Duke's campus and it's me and my black girlfriend and there's a white guy by the Duke wall and he just hollered out 'Nigger' to me and I'm just so angry, I didn't know who to call. I don't know if this is an emergency. They're just hanging out by the wall off of Buchanan Street. It's right in front of 610 Buchanan Street. I saw them all come out of like a big frat house and me and my black girlfriend are walking by and they called us Niggers. . . . I live in a neighborhood where they wrote 'KKK' on the side of a white station wagon and that's near right where I'm at . . . and they didn't harm me in any way. . . . It's right in front of 610 Buchanan, I saw them coming out of this frat house, 610 North

Buchanan, I'm sitting right in front of it right now. I'm not gonna press the issue, but however Durham City feels about racial slurs and stuff . . . however you guys want to handle it. I'm not hurt in any way, okay. Thank you, baby. Bye.

That phone call revealed a third version of events from the two women. The statement contains at least one glaring inconsistency. During this 911 call, Roberts first claimed to be "driving" by the house at 610 North Buchanan, and then stated that she and her girlfriend were "walking" past the house. She also first reported that it was a "white guy" who yelled racial slurs and then expanded that to "they." The obvious conclusion is that one or both of these women were lying.

According to Roberts, after the women drove off, Mangum was "basically out of it." She couldn't even tell Roberts where she lived so she could take her home. Roberts then drove to a local Kroger supermarket and complained to a clerk that there was a woman in her car who wouldn't get out. At 1:22 a.m. the store security guard called 911 and told them, "There's a lady in someone else's car and she would not get out of the car." She also told the police dispatcher that Mangum was "intoxicated or drunk or something."

About ten minutes later, two officers from the Durham Police Department arrived and found Mangum "unconscious" in Roberts's car wearing "one white high-heeled shoe" and a "see-through red outfit" with nothing underneath. One of the officers reported back to a dispatcher that Mangum was "breathing, appears to be fine, she's not in distress, she's just passed out drunk." Officer Sgt. J.C. Shelton tried to awaken Mangum by waving an ammonia capsule under her nose, and she began to breathe through her mouth, leading him to believe that "she was not really unconscious."

Apparently, Mangum refused to answer any questions or identify herself. Since she did not appear to be injured, Officer Shelton had another officer take her to Durham ACCESS, a drug treatment/mental health facility, where Mangum identified herself as "Honey" and stated that she did not want to go to jail. The nurse, thinking that Mangum was confused and unable to think straight, asked her if she had been raped. Mangum responded that she had. The nurse then notified the Durham Police Department, and an officer took Mangum to the Duke University Medical Center emergency room where a sexual assault nurse examiner (SANE) examined her. That was when the police began their investigation into Mangum's allegations that she was raped at the lacrosse house.

I was beginning to perceive a picture that I hadn't heard about on the news. The impression that was generally presented by the media during those first harrowing months following the party was obviously skewed, and the groundwork had been laid for a pretty nasty outcome. There were tales that supported the notion that spring break is all about wet T-shirt contests, girls gone wild, and orgies of drunken teens partying the nights away on Jell-O shots, drugs, and beer. And what happened at Duke initially led to allegations that the party at 610 North Buchanan was typical of those types of bashes, which were further described as being commonplace at elite universities. It was generally reported that this was the kind of typical raucous gathering that one would expect from a bunch of spoiled rich kids who have the cash flow and party-hardy attitudes to get away with just about anything on a campus that regards athletes as though they are among the privileged few who deserve complete run of the place.

According to several of these unsubstantiated reports, this was the impression of the boys that those of us who were out of the loop were expected to believe. Given those images of rowdy behavior and elitist, rich white athletes, some thought it not too surprising how the rest of the evening's events unfolded on March 13, according to the strippers' allegations.

When the investigation into Mangum's allegations commenced, Sgt. Mark Gottlieb was the supervisor. According to several sources, Gottlieb was notorious for his disfavor of Duke students. Some individuals believe his animosity stems from what Gottlieb may perceive as the Duke students' privilege and status. Statistics confirm that Gottlieb has gone out of his way to arrest Duke students, handcuff them, and put them in jail, while nonstudents who have committed the same offenses were treated much more leniently. In fact, bail amounts for the Duke students are substantially greater than those of local suspects under investigation for much more serious crimes and who also posed a flight risk. The area around the house at 610 North Buchanan has also apparently been a thorn in Gottlieb's side for quite awhile: neighbors of the row of houses occupied mostly by Duke students have constantly complained about the students' wild parties. The lacrosse party allegations gave Gottlieb the ammunition he needed to go after the students, while at the same time placating the complaining neighbors.

I met with James F. Coleman, Jr., a Duke Law School professor who served as chief counsel for the U.S. House of Representatives' Committee on Standards of Official Conduct and was former head of a Duke committee to review drug use by athletes. After the allegations, he served as Chair of the Lacrosse Ad Hoc Review Committee formed by Duke University President Richard Brodhead to look into the lacrosse team's disciplinary record.

Coleman was not asked to investigate the criminal allegations. His mission was to examine whether the behavior of lacrosse team members was as distasteful and undesirable as people were claiming after Mangum's accusations were unleashed. Coleman told me that there had been allegations from the District Attorney, the neighbors, and other students that the lacrosse team members were a bunch of hooligans, rapists, and racists, and that they were engaged in all sorts of conduct that the university was covering up. He also concurred with the impression that others had given me that Gottlieb had it in for the team members, as well as Duke students in general. After an extensive investigation, Coleman's committee determined that the alleged problems with the lacrosse team were greatly exaggerated. This case, he believed, typified what happens in a lot of instances—people were using the publicity surrounding the lacrosse team as an opportunity to push their own agendas. In particular, neighbors were utilizing the allegations to bolster their own complaints about problems they had with students who lived in their neighborhood. Although their grievances actually had nothing to do with the lacrosse team, by using Mangum's accusations as just another example of ongoing problems with the players, they were able to attract attention.

Coleman informed me that the police have a "Top Ten List" of the worst houses in the area. Interestingly enough, the house located at 610 North Buchanan, where the lacrosse players lived, is not on that list. He said that from what he had learned, the team members were not even there very often, leading some of the neighbors to believe that the students had moved out. Coleman mentioned that he had included that in his report. He also told me something that I found very interesting under the circumstances: none of the "Top Ten" houses were affiliated with the Duke athletic teams. He said that those houses that were problematic belonged to the fraternities and sororities where the biggest parties were held.

It was obvious that the lacrosse team had been caught in the crossfire of some much bigger issues that had plagued both Duke University as well as the surrounding neighborhood for quite some time. Coleman shed more light on the issue by describing an experience he had while conducting his investigation. He told me that there was a house that had been identified as a lacrosse house, but it was not one of the major sore spots in the neighborhood. However, a member of the city council appeared on television and was quoted in the newspaper castigating the lacrosse houses as a blight upon the neighborhood. Coleman interviewed him and asked, "Okay, tell us what the facts are. Identify the houses." And the councilman said, "You know, I had someone from NBC here and I walked him around the neighborhood and showed him the houses." Coleman responded, "You said these were lacrosse players' houses. So, what I want to know is which one of the houses rented by the lacrosse players was there a problem at?" The councilman answered, "Well, I can't identify the lacrosse house, but these houses were really the problem." Coleman told me that none of the houses the councilman was referring to were lacrosse houses. He added that this was the nature of what was going on. "That man had absolutely no information at all about the lacrosse house, but he had made reference to it as though he knew it was a problem."

"People were just using these kids," Coleman told me. "I don't think they intended to harm them. Their view was, they wanted the university to do something about the problems they were having in the neighborhood, and if they could get them to do that by jumping onto the lacrosse team-bashing bandwagon, then that's what they did. And they were totally indifferent to the impact it would have on the lacrosse team, or the players, or the students. They just didn't care. It was selfish."

Coleman said his committee found nothing that would distinguish the lacrosse players from other students. He shared his thoughts with me about that:

Among athletes they did have a higher percentage of disciplinary citations, but we pointed out in the report that that was due to the lacrosse culture, which is that they are a very tight group of guys, they do things in groups, and they don't spread out to other groups. So that when somebody is in the dormitory making noise or drinking beer and it's a lacrosse player, just about everybody else in the room is a lacrosse player. That's not true of football players or basketball players who do things with other students. The lacrosse players know each other before they come here because they're recruited from a small number of schools. So, from the day they get here, they have a built-in social group. And that's a big factor in the number of citations. In terms of the nature of citations, they were no different than the kinds of things other students were doing. They were not involved in assaults, sexual offenses, or racist conduct. We didn't find any of that.

Coleman added that he believed that people who were vying to get attention for their issues knew that if they somehow connected them with the lacrosse team, they would get the cameras to show up.

I couldn't help but think about how Coleman's description of things was in line with the information that I had heard from others. My focus of the lacrosse incident was drifting further away from the team members and more toward those who may have been utilizing it for their own agendas. My outrage grew at the thought that those boys might have been made into scapegoats at the whim of a bunch of agenda-ridden radicals.

I had already compiled an enormous amount of information, but I continued to gather details to determine whether there was a pattern. I met with Bob Ekstrand again and sat down to ask him about certain information I had received. He concurred that the problem was not really about the lacrosse players and commented that there was much more to this whole incident than meets the eye.

He described his own experience with the allegations against the lacrosse team. As it turned out, Bob's paralegal, Stefanie Sparks, had played for the women's lacrosse team at Duke, and she was currently involved with the women's team as an assistant coach. Stefanie was friends with many of the guys on the men's lacrosse team and was very fond of them. Within days after the alleged incident took place, Bob and Stefanie heard that the team was planning to go down to the police station voluntarily to answer one or two questions and that Gottlieb was in charge of the investigation. Bob had serious concerns about this prospect. His fear was that if police believed a rape had taken place, they would do everything they could to sort out who the principals and accomplices were. In other words, the boys would meet with the police, they would be separated and interrogated, and each one would be told, "Everybody else is giving a DNA sample voluntarily, so why don't you?" In short, what was going to happen was exactly what happened to the three captains. They were separated and asked questions. Then they requested a polygraph, but the police told them they wouldn't do it; they just wanted the DNA. The captains offered to do both. But the police still refused to administer the polygraph.

This was an extremely serious situation. The boys were looking at charges of first-degree forcible rape, first-degree sexual offense, and kidnapping. According to Bob, "There's not a judge in the state that won't boxcar the sentences; the boys will serve their sentences consecutively." He considered it a "de facto life sentence," meaning that even though they wouldn't technically be sentenced to "life in prison," the amount of years they would serve if convicted would just about equal it.

The other troubling issue was that if the alleged crimes had actually occurred, anybody who admitted being at the party could conceivably be indicted along with the principals as aiders and abettors. Bob explained that "the North Carolina law for accomplice liability is stretched beyond all proportions and it covers just about anybody. If you're on the scene, there is probable cause to arrest you as a lookout."

Bob said that Dean Wasiolek had spoken to Dan Flannery and suggested that the boys go down to the police station and do whatever the police ask and not tell their parents. Then Coach Pressler announced to the boys that they would be going to the police station the next day to be questioned about the party. He told them to keep it in house. He was operating under the impression that this was a simple matter of telling the truth and the issue would go away. Dean Wasiolek had essentially told him that. That was the undercurrent, and most of the boys thought that if they didn't talk about it, the whole thing would die down.

The night before the boys were supposed to speak with the police, Bob asked them what they were being questioned about and they still didn't know. They were not aware of the magnitude of what was happening. The party had been on Monday, March 13 and the search of 610 North Buchanan had taken place on Thursday, March 16. According to Bob, most of the lacrosse players didn't even know about the seriousness of the situation until they read the school newspaper, *The Chronicle*, on Monday, March 20.

"We now know through discovery that the one or two questions the boys were supposed to answer were not one or two questions," Bob told me.

The police had, in fact, corralled numerous crime scene forensic folks to deal with forty-six suspects and take DNA and the rest. The boys were going to walk into a full-blown interrogation. And you can only imagine what the police would have done. We have already seen what they do with witness statements. They were going to sit down with these boys and not only were they going to run them up against each other with no ground rules, a free for all, but none of them would have even had the benefit of a conversation with their parents.

Bob made a decision to intervene and do what Stefanie had been sug-
gesting for several days: see to it that the boys discussed the situation
with their parents before talking to police. Stefanie got word to the
lacrosse players about what the couple of questions really meant and
instructed them to tell their parents, because, as Bob stated, "it is the
most dangerous thing in the world to talk to the police for as serious
a crime as this without the benefit of counsel."

Bob laid out how he thought the interrogation would have gone.

> The issue was that the police were going to say to each boy,
> 'There was a rape in this house and you know it.' And the boy
> will say, 'You're wrong, you're absolutely wrong, officer. I know
> for a fact that no rape occurred. I know it because I was there
> the whole time, and if something happened while I was there,
> I would know. You can't do something like that in that small
> house without everybody knowing.' And, in that way, each boy
> would be implicating himself and sealing his own fate.

Bob suggested that the boys postpone the questioning in order to have
a chance to discuss it with their parents. After that, all sorts of misrep-
resentations went out to the media, such as that the boys refused to
answer any questions and that they had lawyered up. Apparently, the
police were furious that the questioning was postponed because,
according to Bob, "they had to move heaven and earth to get ready for
their grand interrogation." In other words, they were preparing to send
the lambs to the slaughter.

2

THE PLOT THICKENS

M angum's second photo identification session took place on March 21, 2006, at which time two photo arrays, all containing only pictures of lacrosse players, were shown to Mangum twice. David Evans's picture was included with those photos, but Mangum did not identify *any* of the people, including Evans, as one of her attackers. When asked if she could remember any further details of her assailants, she stated that she could not.

The two photo identification sessions that had thus far been administered to Mangum were overseen by an investigator who was not involved in the case. He informed Mangum that "the person who committed the crime may or may not be included." He also told her that he did not know whether the person who committed the crime was included. She was informed that "things like hair styles, beards, and mustaches can be easily changed and that complexion colors may look slightly different in the photographs." More importantly, she was told, "You should not feel like you have to make an identification." These are important safeguards necessary to prevent bias during the identification process.

But there was a procedural problem with the photo arrays. "Fillers" were not used, meaning that for every picture of a suspect contained in an array, Mangum should have been shown five pictures of non-suspects to keep from unfairly pointing her toward anyone known to be a possible suspect. At least some of the verbal safeguards required during an identification session were in place. But, as you will see shortly, that soon changed.

By the time Wes Covington had arranged to meet with the team, the three lacrosse captains, David Evans, Dan Flannery, and Matt Zash, had already voluntarily gone down to have their DNA tested, give their statements, and have their mug shots taken without legal representation. On March 23, 2006, ten days after the party, Sgt. Gottlieb called Wes's associate, Andy Peterson, to arrange for the rest of the team to go down and give samples of their DNA and have their mug shots taken. Gottlieb complained that he was being pressured by the D.A.'s office to get the players down there sooner rather than later to document any scratch marks the boys might have that would be consistent with what the victim said she did to them when she allegedly fought back. The problem, according to Wes, was that the boys are all lacrosse players. Lacrosse is a sport that involves constant physical contact among the players, and there were going to be bruises and scratches all over them anyway.

Wes was already scheduled to meet with Coach Pressler and the lacrosse team that day. Right before he left for the meeting, Gottlieb called to inform him that he was going to obtain a non-testimonial identification order (NTO). An NTO is an order of the court that can be acquired prior to arrest, after an arrest, or virtually anytime, wherein the court orders someone to deliver something. Usually the order would seek DNA samples, hair samples, saliva, or whatever else is relevant to a case. This one required DNA samples as well as photographs to be taken of forty-six Duke lacrosse players. The one black team member, Devon Sherwood, was excluded from the order since the complainant said her alleged assailants were white.

NTOs usually allow for a seventy-two-hour window, which gives a defendant time to hire an attorney and present the evidence that the court ordered. But it can be within whatever time limit the court requires, and this particular one was for that day at 4:00 p.m. Wes headed out to meet with Pressler and the team and wait for the NTO to arrive. In an effort to avoid exposing the boys to a media frenzy, Wes arranged with Gottlieb to have them go to a location where they weren't likely to encounter the press, rather than the main police station. They agreed on a crime lab that was located in a less conspicuous place. Prior to going down to the lab, Wes addressed the members of the lacrosse team. He told them that he had already met with Dan, Matt, and David, and he was there to discuss their options. He explained that he had the NTO and that they had to obey it. He also said that, in his opinion, they did not need lawyers yet, that they were going down to give samples for something that did not occur, and as long as it did not occur, they had nothing to worry about. He added, "If any of you know to the contrary, then you should get lawyers, but so long as you didn't do anything and didn't see anything, you have nothing to worry about." Wes gave them the address and directions and told them he and Andy would meet them there.

Bob Ekstrand also spoke with the team before they left for the crime lab. He told the players that he would make sure the NTO was authentic and signed by a judge. He also told the players that he had significant doubts about whether any order compelling forty-six individuals to produce DNA samples was sufficiently particularized enough for each individual to pass constitutional muster. He imagined a five hundred-page document would be required to establish the particularized probable cause needed for each individual listed. While everyone waited for the NTO to be transmitted by fax to the Murray Building offices, Bob said he would walk the boys through their options. If the order was valid on its face, they would have to comply with it or move to quash it on the substantive grounds that it was overbroad. He offered to talk to each one individually if they wished, and told them their parents could be included in the discussion by phone; then the fax came in. Much lighter than he expected (only a handful of pages), Bob told me that when he saw Judge Stevens's signature on the NTO, he knew it was a valid order issued by a judge he knew to be fair and straightforward. His doubts about the constitutional validity grew, however, when he saw that an order for all forty-six boys was supported by a single affidavit. The particularized probable cause for each individual, it appeared, amounted to a mere two things: (1) being white, and (2) being a member of the Duke University's Men's Lacrosse Team. He told the boys that the NTO was signed by Judge Stevens, and, as such, it appeared, on its face, to be a valid order. Before he could begin walking the team members through their options, all of them ran out to their cars and headed for the lab.

The boys were anxious to do this because, like Bob, they saw DNA testing as the answer that would end this nightmare. On the surface, they were correct in their thinking, because, as Bob commented, "anyone who read the affidavit in support of the NTO would assume that if the rape it describes actually occurred, the rape kit would be so covered with DNA, that it would glow." Since they knew that no rape or assault had occurred, it was reasonable for the boys to believe that they would be cleared when the DNA test results came back negative. In light of the violent sexual assault that the affidavit described, Bob agreed. He remembered thinking, for these boys, "this case will begin and end with DNA."

Wes and Andy arrived at the testing facility ahead of the boys, and Wes confronted Gottlieb, asking why he had obtained the order when the boys were already willing to go in voluntarily. Gottlieb responded that he had been told by the D.A.'s office that he had to get the order. He also said that the boys were submitting to DNA testing in order to rule out innocent persons. And that is what everyone believed because when applying for the NTO, District Attorney Mike Nifong's office stated in the application that "the DNA evidence . . . will immediately rule out any innocent persons, and show conclusive evidence as to who the suspect(s) are in the alleged violent attack upon this victim."

When the forty-six lacrosse team members arrived at the lab, the press snapped pictures of them with their coats covering their heads. While trying to hide the identity of an innocent person is not good PR, under the circumstances it seemed to make some sense. The boys did not do it instinctively; they did it at the direction of Bob Ekstrand's paralegal, Stefanie Sparks. Mangum, Stefanie feared, would see them on television and, when looking at the photos, would identify them as her alleged attackers—intentionally or not—based on this television viewing. Stefanie believed that she was protecting them. As it turned out, she was right. Thus far, Mangum had not identified any of the boys as her attackers. Had Mangum been given an opportunity to see the boys' faces on television when they were entering the crime lab, she would have had the opportunity to study them and perhaps claim that some of the boys were her attackers.

On March 24, 2006, the day after the NTO was carried out, Durham District Attorney Mike Nifong took over the case. It was an unusual move for a D.A. to take charge of a case prior to an arrest having been made.

At this point, as mentioned earlier, the lacrosse captains, Zash, Flannery, and Evans, had voluntarily given statements, had their pictures taken, submitted DNA samples, and even offered to take polygraphs. They were also fully cooperative in helping the police execute the search warrant on their house, and they freely turned over their laptops and cell phones. The remaining lacrosse team members also eagerly complied with the NTO in the hopes that their full cooperation, combined with the DNA test results that they knew would be negative, would bring an end to the nightmare they were experiencing. Yet, in spite of the fact that the players went out of their way to be fully cooperative and forthcoming, as soon as Nifong took charge of the case, he began making outrageously false and inflammatory public statements that reflected just the opposite. For example, he insisted that the team members were not cooperating with authorities. He told NBC 17 News that the "lacrosse team members were standing together and refusing to talk with investigators." He commented to a reporter for ABC 11 TV News that "[m]y only guess is that some of this stonewall of silence that we have seen may tend to crumble once charges start to come out." He even went so far as to add that he "might bring aiding-and-abetting charges against some of the players who were not cooperating." Additionally, while being interviewed by a representative from CNN, Nifong stated that "[i]t just seems like a shame that they are not willing to violate this seeming sacred sense of loyalty to team for loyalty to community." These statements were all made before the end of March 2006 and within one week after Nifong took over the case, and they did a great deal of damage to the Duke students' standing in public opinion. The implications made the situation look very dark, especially when combined with the contents of the 911 phone call from Roberts on March 14 that was already circulating. And as Nifong fed members of the media inflammatory statements, they went into a feeding frenzy.

The damning comments from Nifong worsened. Most people could not conceive of the fact that the District Attorney could or even *would* make official statements about a case unless he had the clear evidence to back them up. Many individuals jumped on the bandwagon and made judgments about the lacrosse players based on what they were hearing from the District Attorney without even realizing that his behavior was totally inappropriate, especially under the circumstances of this case. The remarks Nifong made were so incriminating that they took the focus off of the one very important issue: Nifong was not doing his job. The main objective for a prosecutor is to seek the truth and achieve justice. If a prosecutor does his job properly, he will protect the innocent—whether is it the alleged victim, the alleged suspects, or anyone else involved in a case. While the American justice system is not perfect, it is still the greatest system in the world. Within this system, there is supposed to be a presumption of innocence, meaning that a suspect is innocent until proven guilty. Due process requires that everyone be guaranteed his or her day in court and the right to a fair trial. Such a requirement is a fundamental part of our democratic system. The problem with this case was that Nifong was doing everything he could to convict the team members in and through the media. His outrageously incriminating statements about the suspects not only totally ignored these boys' fundamental rights and completely tainted and prejudiced the judicial process, but they also fueled the fire of those who were using the issue to gain ground with their own agendas. Nifong's actions were so shockingly inappropriate that I wondered what he stood to benefit by going after the lacrosse team.

Wes Covington has known Nifong for a long time, and his perspective provided me with a clearer picture of the man. Wes met him as a kid when they were both students at L.J. Bell Elementary in Rockingham, North Carolina. They even worked in the school store together. Wes said he lost track of Nifong and ran into him again in 1981 while Wes was in law school taking a clinical course in criminal litigation. As part of the program, he was an intern at the Durham D.A.'s office where Nifong worked. After graduation, Wes was offered a position as an assistant district attorney and worked there for seven years until approximately 1987. He said that Nifong was probably one of the better prosecutors as far as trying cases, but that his actions outside the courtroom were much different. "As he tries cases," Wes explained, "he's emotionally reserved, which is appropriate. In his personal life, and in his interactions with other lawyers, he's the complete opposite." Wes described Nifong as someone who could be "relatively charming. However, if he doesn't need you, he is dismissive." For example, Wes told me about an incident that took place with a student involved in the Duke undergraduate mock trial that he advises. One intern of Nifong's recollected Nifong's rather harsh response to another intern. The new intern extended his hand toward Nifong when introduced to him. Nifong looked him in the face and said, "I don't shake hands with interns." Wes also said that "Nifong takes any challenge to his position on any issue regarding virtually anything, as a personal affront and that once Nifong holds a grudge, he never lets it go."

Some people, citing the fact that Nifong graduated from UNC-Chapel Hill Law School, think his campaign against the lacrosse players stems from his hatred for his alma mater's biggest rival, Duke. Perhaps his animosity toward Duke has more to do with the fact that it is his own parents' alma mater. However, Wes attributed Nifong's crusade to something else: his "obsession to win an election against a bitter rival, Freda Black." I didn't understand how Freda Black could have had anything to do with Nifong's overly aggressive attack on the lacrosse team regarding Crystal Mangum's claim of an alleged rape. But Wes explained:

> Freda Black was an assistant D.A. with Nifong under District Attorney Jim Hardin. Freda and Nifong vied for Jim's approval. And whomever Hardin would tend to listen to, the other one would get bent out of shape. Hardin went to Governor Easley and said, "I want you to appoint Mike as my successor." Nifong had been in the D.A.'s Office from around 1980 until now. So his retirement with the state is close to fully vested. Vested with the State of North Carolina is thirty years. At the time Nifong was appointed by the Governor, he was a wholly apolitical individual. In fact, he disliked politics. He always told people, "I'm

happy doing what I'm doing," and if he'd stayed in what he was doing, we wouldn't be in this mess today. The Governor agreed to appoint Nifong, much later publicly stating that it was on the condition that he not run in the next election. Freda was still under Nifong as an assistant D.A. Very soon after his appointment, Nifong took Freda's parking space under the courthouse away, a very small and tacky thing to do. Naturally, Freda complained about it and Nifong fired her. Freda did the unthinkable in Nifong's eyes: She went to work for an attorney named Jerry Clayton who had a local firm that essentially handles district court traffic and criminal cases.

Apparently, back when Jim Hardin was running for D.A., his opposition was Pat Evans, a black woman whose campaign Jerry Clayton and his group had funded. Of course, this didn't sit well with Nifong. He hated Freda Black already, and now he thinks she has gone to work for the enemy. All defense lawyers in Nifong's eyes are the enemy. I've seen him run out of the courtroom yelling 'Goddamn defense lawyers! Goddamn defense lawyers!'

But, according to Wes, "going to work for the enemy was not Nifong's biggest gripe with Freda. He said that very shortly after taking the job with Clayton, Freda announced that she was going to be a candidate in the upcoming election for district attorney. Nifong found out that Freda was going to run against him and she had the financial backing that he didn't have, so he knew that he had a problem in the election." Wes explained:

Nifong wasn't well-known or popular with the local political groups, Durham Voters Alliance, Durham People's Alliance, and the Committee on the Affairs of Black People, and the Committee on the Affairs of Black People is one of the most efficient political organizations in the United States. They can endorse somebody and guarantee a certain number of votes, because they literally hand out ballots to anyone who can vote and it works. The other two organizations were very liberal. They didn't care for Nifong. His chances of being elected from the moment that Freda said she would run were very bad, especially since she had made somewhat of a name for herself when she prosecuted a very high profile murder case in 2003. The other candidate, a black attorney named Keith Bishop, was a threat to Nifong's ability to get the black vote. Nifong scrambled around and went to the old powers that be in Durham County democratic politics to start lining up people for money. Those who didn't endorse Freda started sending contributions to Nifong. Even so, Freda outspent him.

But Wes believes that "Nifong was able to get the Committee on the Affairs of Black People's endorsement because of the lacrosse case. He said Nifong hung on to that case and used it as his ticket to gain their support." All along, it was obvious to many observers that Nifong—who is white—was pursuing the lacrosse case in order to win favor from black voters. Duke Law School Professor James Coleman, during an appearance on *60 Minutes,* stated, "I think that [Nifong] pandered to the [black] community by saying, 'I'm gonna go out there and defend your interests in seeing that these hooligans who committed the crime are prosecuted. I'm not gonna let their fathers, with all of their money, buy . . . big-time lawyers and get them off. I'm doing this for you.'" Coleman continued, "You know, what are you to conclude about a prosecutor who says to you, 'I'll do whatever it takes to get this set of defendants'? What does it say about what he's willing to do to get poor black defendants?" A former ardent supporter of Nifong's, African American attorney Floyd McKissick, a Duke Law School alumnus who serves as chairperson of the Durham Democratic Party, obviously agrees with Coleman. In an April 2, 2007, *Newsday* article entitled "Duke D.A. Backlash," McKissick was quoted as saying that "The African American community of Durham wants fairness, and the view is that if Mr. Nifong was not fair in this case, what's he going to be like in other cases?"

At the time of the so-called "conspiracy of silence" that Nifong was falsely reporting about the lacrosse players, Bob Ekstrand was advising all forty-six players in the "suspect group." He notified Gottlieb that, going forward, he would either assist the boys in finding independent counsel, or he would represent them himself in a common defense arrangement if they chose to go that route. Bob told Gottlieb that, if he wanted to speak to any of the lacrosse team members, he should contact Ekstrand himself. If Bob was continuing his representation of the individual, then they would discuss Gottlieb's request; if Bob had obtained independent counsel for the individual, he would provide that information to Gottlieb. Bob said that for most of the pre-indictment period, he represented roughly forty of the boys, with five or six being represented jointly by himself and another lawyer, and never once did he receive a call from Gottlieb requesting an interview. The only request the police lodged with Bob's office was an eleventh-hour plea for any information that might establish who was not at the party. Bob told me that the police were clearly afraid that Nifong would indict someone that we would be able to prove was not even in the state of North Carolina at the time.

Over and over again in my quest for truth in this case, I heard about the utter lack of communication between the police department and the boys or their representatives. It was a consistent pattern among all of the people in charge of investigating Mangum's allegations. I had suspected that to be the case, but I did not know how far it extended until I heard about the details behind the creation of Bob and Stefanie's timeline detailing the events of the night of March 13 and the early morning hours of March 14, 2006. (See Appendix.)

While the boys were being impeached as witnesses and portrayed in a mostly negative light in the press, Bob and Stefanie spent several days building a timeline of the events in question. They put together their knowledge of each player's whereabouts on the evening of March 13 and compared them to the timestamps on the photos taken at the party as well as the contents of the photos themselves. Bob decided that, for purposes of turning the public perception around, they could only use independently corroborated evidence. And they found plenty of it! The photos taken at the party contained a wealth of information. For one thing, the metadata files showing when the digital pictures were created allowed Bob and Stefanie to determine when the dance started (midnight); what time the dance ended (12:03:57 a.m.); and most importantly, what time the boys got Mangum into Kim's car before the two finally departed (12:41:32 a.m.).

The timestamps in the metadata file for each picture were crucial, so Bob quickly retained a forensics expert to examine the computer files and the camera. The expert was to determine whether the metadata files were altered or tampered with at all, and to create a forensic copy of all of the digital photos in the event they were needed at a trial. The computer forensics expert confirmed that the pictures and their metadata files had not been altered in any way.

Because Bob knew the public might be skeptical about a retained forensics expert vouching for the integrity of the metadata, he told Stefanie they needed something else to corroborate the timestamps. Stefanie poured over the pictures for hours looking for something. She found it in the wristwatch of one of the partygoers pictured. Stefanie saw that the time on the watch clearly corresponded with the timestamps on the pictures. That was just what Bob was looking for; it was corroboration that anyone could evaluate for themselves.

Bob knew that the pictures and their metadata would be a rock-solid foundation upon which all forty-six players could build their proof of innocence. If anyone were to be indicted, Bob knew that the combination of the pictures along with that individual's transaction records, cell phone calls, and dorm keycard swipes would be a means of quickly establishing the truth. Bob also knew that the array of data could be assembled in no time, and would be immediately available to deflect the traditional public response to news of an indictment. In one news cycle, the story could change from "Lacrosse Player Indicted" to "Indicted Lacrosse Player in Dorm at Time of Alleged Rape" or variations on that theme.

To further corroborate the times, they took a statement from Jason Alexander Bissey who lived next door to 610 North Buchanan Bloulevard and compared the information in his statement to the timestamps on the pictures. Amazingly, Bissey had keyed in on the time throughout that fateful night of March 13 and his recollection of what was happening next door during those times has played an essential role in impeaching Mangum's claims. In a statement prepared for the police, Bissey, who lived at 608 North Buchanan Bloulevard, was able to lay out a timeline that corresponded exactly with the time-stamped photos that the lacrosse players had snapped before, during, and shortly after the party. According to Bissey, at approximately 2:00 p.m. on March 13, as he left his house, he noticed the guys next door in the backyard playing "washers and drinking beers." He said he "returned to [his] residence at approximately 11:30 p.m." and saw "some of the men still lingering in the backyard." He said that he saw two women, appearing to be African American, heading toward 610 North Buchanan. Bissey described the apparel that they were wearing. "One . . . was dressed in an extremely short tan skirt and was wearing high heels. . . . The other woman was more conservatively dressed in pants and a sweater. . . ." From everything I had learned, Roberts was the one in the conservative outfit and Mangum arrived dressed to dance. Soon, Bissey noticed the women alone in the yard. At around midnight, he observed the women going into the house. "At approximately 12:05 a.m. Tuesday" (now March 14, 2006), Bissey entered his house and showered. When he finished, he "heard loud voices outside." Sometime between "12:20 a.m. and 12:30 a.m." Bissey "observed twenty to thirty young men in the alley between the two houses and on the sidewalk in front of [his] build-ing." They were yelling about money. One of the guys was talking to someone through the driver's side window of a car parked out front. Everything seemed to calm down and Bissey heard some of the young men repeatedly saying, "Guys, let's go." At approximately 12:30 a.m. he noticed the more scantily dressed woman, (Mangum) go back to the house saying something about retrieving her shoe. He commented, "She seemed agitated, not hysterical." Within fifteen to twenty min-utes, at approximately 1:00 a.m., he heard another commotion and noticed a car speed away and the guys heading toward Duke's East Campus. He said that the party appeared to be over.

Bissey's information was also consistent with the time that Roberts had made the call to 911 as she was about to pull away from the house at 610 North Buchanan. It was recorded as coming in at 12:53 a.m. By 1:22 a.m., the Kroger security guard, Angel Altmon, had contacted police to get Mangum out of Roberts's car. So the timeline was taking shape, and there were other significant details that fit nicely into it. Some of the boys had airtight alibis that also corresponded with the timeline.

That information was substantial in terms of corroboration, but there was more. Officer Himan's affidavit in support of the NTO stated that Mangum claimed that while she was being beaten and raped, in an effort to save herself, she fought back, resulting in some of her artificial nails being ripped off. The alleged loss of the nails proved to be some of the most damaging evidence to the accuser's case. The police found them at the scene during their search of the premises. However, when Bob and Stefanie zoomed in on the photos of Mangum that showed her hands, they were able to clearly see that several of her nails were already missing while she was dancing with Roberts and before any of the alleged rape and assault supposedly took place. In fact, not only could they see that the nails were missing during Mangum's performance, there were other pictures that showed the bathroom sink with four nails neatly lined up on it. Those photos were taken after the fact, actually, after the police had performed their search of the premises. Strangely, the police had left those nails behind during their search and only seized the ones that the boys had picked out of the bathroom garbage can for them. Bob came up with a pretty good theory as to what he thought had happened. He suggested that Mangum might have been expecting to put her nails on when she arrived at the party. Since she was late, she didn't have time to finish, so they were left behind on the sink and the boys didn't touch them.

The pictures also revealed something else that was very interesting. While Mangum was dancing, she had several bruises on her body. Of course, the pictures were taken well before any of the alleged rape and assault were said to have taken place. Bob and Stefanie assumed that they were the "marks of a woman who lives a hard life." Later, they found out that Mangum claimed that her alleged attackers had inflicted those bruises during the alleged attack.

On two separate occasions, prior to any action being taken by the university, Bob and Stefanie offered the timeline and corroborating evidence to Duke administrators. They had been advising most of the team members at the time, and they cared enough about Duke and the boys to try to head off any serious actions being taken against them by the school. However, Duke's officials declined to meet with them to review the evidence.

Just as the story was breaking, parents of the players, along with Bob, had talked to members of the Duke administration who report to University President Richard Brodhead and said,

> We're not asking Duke to support the team. We would love you to, but we understand the pressures. We are just asking that you don't say or do anything to hurt the boys, because you might not realize what will actually hurt them right now. So, why don't you run by us what you propose to do and we won't talk about it with anyone, but we'll help you from making a terrible mistake.

Bob's motivation for approaching the Duke administration was to attempt to keep the controversy in check rather than allow them to make the situation worse through their potential public condemnation. During his discussion with Duke, Bob said,

> In particular, do not get so far away from the boys with a statement that you can't come back from, because you will want to come back. At the end of the day, these boys are innocent. You don't have to take anyone's word for it; the DNA tests will demonstrate it. When the truth comes out, you will want to know that you did not abandon them or visibly distance yourself from them. If you remain neutral now and do nothing to condemn these boys, you will probably draw criticism, but it will not be long before you will be lauded for your ability to withstand the pressures that are on you now. They will not be on you for long, and the DNA tests will come back and exonerate these boys.

Bob first communicated this to a Duke administrator on March 27 and again a short time later. His goal was to influence Richard

Brodhead to refrain from making substantive comments on the allegations or the boys until the investigation was concluded and all the facts were known. In order to provide the assurances he thought President Brodhead would need, he told administrators he would walk them through the timeline and corroborating evidence. The answer Bob received was that "Brodhead doesn't need that." At that point in time, Brodhead was still trying to decide whether to kill the team's season by suspending the rest of the lacrosse games.

On Sunday, March 26, 2006, several protesters, including Duke students, organized a demonstration in front of 610 North Buchanan where they held signs that read, "You can't rape and run," "It's Sunday morning, time to confess," "Give them equal measure," "Castrate!!," "Outraged Duke Alum," "Get a conscience, not a lawyer," and "Real men tell the truth." Speakers holding bullhorns shouted threats meant for the lacrosse players, such as "The community consequences for this action will range far beyond the legal consequences that you will face." And then there were the "Potbangers," members of the campus and neighboring community who demonstrated by banging in unison on pots and drums, chanting the following words that had been distributed in a handout:

> Who's being Silent?
> They're being silent!
> Whose[sic] protecting rapists?
> They're protecting rapist[s]!
> So, who are the rapists?
> They must be the rapists!
> Out of the house!
> Out of the town!
> We don't want,
> You around!

I've seen the videos of the protests held that day. I will never forget the sights and sounds. I cannot even imagine what it would have been like for the boys to have been subjected to those atrocities had they still been residing in the house. I am appalled that there was such an overwhelming rush to judgment, especially on the part of some who were the team members' peers. But that was just the beginning.

On March 27, 2006, Ruth Sheehan, a staff writer for the North Carolina newspaper, *News & Observer*, wrote an article that was posted on www.newsobserver.com entitled "Team's Silence Is Sickening." The following is what Sheehan wrote, in part:

Members of the Duke men's lacrosse team: You know.

We know you know.

What happened in the bathroom at the stripper party gone terribly terribly bad, you know who was involved. Every one of you does.

And one of you needs to come forward and tell the police.

Do not be afraid of retribution on the team. Do not be persuaded that somehow this "happened" to one or more "good guys."

If what the strippers say is true—that one of them was raped, sodomized, beaten and strangled—the guys responsible are not "good."

This seems an elementary statement, I know.

But I can see loyal team members sitting around convincing themselves that it would be disloyal to turn on their teammates—why, the guys who were involved were just a little "over the top." In real life, they're funny. They call their mothers once a week. They share class notes with friends. They attend church.

On this night, they were just a little too drunk, a little too "worked up." It was a scene straight out of "I am Charlotte Simmons" by Tom Wolfe. Indicative of the times. The alleged racial epithets slung at the strippers, who were black?

Is Sheehan asking readers a rhetorical question to make some sort of point? If so, what exactly is it? Further on in her article, she continued with her imagined scenario:

> I can see the team going down this path, justifying its silence. And it makes me sick.
>
> Because, of all the occupational hazards that must come with stripping, one of them should not be rape. And no, forced sex by a hunky prep student doesn't make it better.
>
> Unfortunately, because the team members are students at such a fine university, there is a tendency to presume that this was an aberration. That these players are "good guys."

Sheehan persisted with futile attempts to make it appear as though she wasn't quite sure if an attack had occurred while at the same time pointing out all of the characteristics of the athletes that would make a rape seem almost inevitable. In no part of the column did Sheehan contemplate the possibility that the strippers had concocted their stories. Was it easier for Sheehan to berate the privileged white athletes without fear of repercussion rather than to enter into a messy and politically incorrect diatribe on the scenario of African American strippers conspiring in the bathroom to take the white boys for their money? Instead, Sheehan rambled on with her questionable punctuation, poor use of sentence structure, and damning comments in an apparent effort to influence team members to come forward and "tell the truth." And where was the word "alleged" in her article? I found it in only one place, right before "racial epithets." There was nothing about the "alleged rape." Sheehan wasn't on the fence. She had climbed over it to stand with the strippers on the side of presumed guilt less than two weeks after the allegations had been made. Just in case there is any doubt about Sheehan's lack of impartiality, one need only read further down in her article to recognize the righteous indignation behind her words.

Her final sentences say it all: "Every member of the men's lacrosse team knows who was involved, whether it was gang rape or not. Until the team members come forward with that information, suspending games is not enough. Shut down the team."

Sheehan wanted those Duke athletes to pay for an allegation, whether or not there was any truth to it. They had already adamantly denied that it happened. What more could they do? Her disgusting display of rush-to-judgment assumption of guilt immediately stomped on the notion that the boys have a constitutional right to the presumption of innocence until and unless they are proven guilty in a court of law, rather than in Sheehan's court of public opinion. However, she was not alone in her "lynch mob" mentality.

On Tuesday, March 28, 2006, many other members of the campus community began demanding that immediate action be taken against the lacrosse team. Hundreds of students joined in a verbal lynching of the boys during "Sexual Assault Prevention Week" as they gathered for a "Take Back the Night" event that was already scheduled before the allegations against the lacrosse players were made. Handing out "Wanted" posters bearing forty-three team members' pictures with the words "PLEASE COME FORWARD" in large print at the top, students demanded that lacrosse players tell the truth about what happened on the night in question. Also on the posters were the following words:

THE PLOT THICKENS

WE'RE NOT SAYING THAT ALL 46 WERE INVOLVED. BUT WE
DO KNOW THAT SOME OF THE PLAYERS INSIDE THAT HOUSE
ON THAT EVENING KNEW WHAT TRANSPIRED AND WE NEED
THEM TO COME FORWARD.
DURHAM POLICE CPL. DAVID ADDISON.
PLEASE CALL DURHAM CRIMESTOPPERS AT 683-1200.
CALLERS MAY REMAIN ANONYMOUS.

At the bottom of the page underneath the photos was this explanation
of why the entire team's photos were not on the poster: "Note: There
are four more players that were not retrieved from the GoDuke.com
website before Duke took down the lacrosse team's roster on Monday
morning, March 27th."

I've tried to understand the logic behind the poster and I can't.
What was the point? The boys weren't fugitives on the run. None of
them had "left town." The poster offered no reward, and there were no
warnings about them being "armed and dangerous." What could the
purpose have been other than to inflame and incite others against the
team? And it may have worked. On that same day, President Brodhead
announced the suspension of the lacrosse team's season pending further investigation into the rape allegations. Also on that day, all four
lacrosse team captains met with Brodhead to express their regret for
having the party that resulted in so much "anguish for the Duke community and shame to [their] families and [themselves]." And they
stated "unequivocally that any allegation that a sexual assault or rape
occurred is totally and transparently false."

On that same day, presumably in accordance with the information
that he had received from David Evans, Investigator Himan met with
one of the a non-lacrosse players who attended the party, a white male
named Blake Boehmler. Boehmler confirmed that he and another

47

white male, a non-lacrosse player named Brent Saeli, had been at 610 North Buchanan Boulevard on the night of March 13, 2006.

But, something else much more important occurred on March 28, 2006: The State Bureau of Investigation (SBI) Crime Lab determined that there was no seminal fluid on or in Mangum's clothing, vagina, rectum, or mouth; no blood, foreign pubic hairs, head hairs, body hairs, or fibers on her clothing or on her person; and no blood in her vagina, rectum, or mouth, making it extremely unlikely that DNA would be found in the samples taken. Nifong was fully aware of those results. However, on March 30, 2006, he stated to the press that he "would not be surprised if condoms were used. Probably an exotic dancer would not be your first choice for unprotected sex" (*Charlotte Observer*, March 29, 2006), even though he had to be well aware from reading the SANE nurse's report that Mangum had stated that her alleged assailants "did not use a condom." Amazingly, Nifong further commented publicly that "the statements that [the team members make] are inconsistent with the physical evidence in this case. . . . They don't want to admit the enormity of what they have done" (*New York Times*, March 30, 2006). Nifong's other comments suggested that the lacrosse team members committed a rape even though he knew that the DNA evidence would not support those claims.

Then, on March 31, 2006, Nifong again misrepresented the facts by making the following comment to a reporter for MSNBC: "If a condom were used, then we might expect that there would not be any DNA evidence recovered from, say, a vaginal swab."

Still apparently determined to find evidence against the lacrosse team members, Nifong refused to allow the SBI results to rule out the forty-six players as suspects in the alleged rape as his office had publicly promised. Instead, on April 5, 2006, Nifong obtained an order to bring the DNA samples and rape kit to another lab, DNA Security, Inc. (DSI), for more sophisticated "Y-STR" chromosome testing, meaning that the only characteristics lifted from an evidentiary item or from a reference sample would be male. What is interesting is that Nifong's attitude was completely inconsistent with his past handling of rape cases. According to an article called "Nifong: DNA 'Excludes' (Except When It Doesn't)" posted on Durham-in-Wonderland, a well-known blog that has been tracking the lacrosse allegations, Nifong, in a 2000 rape case, "maintained that since DNA evidence trumped witness identifications, DNA tests could—*and should*—exclude the falsely accused." According to the article, there were two rapes in the Trinity Park neighborhood by Duke's East Campus in 2000. Pressure from residents in the area forced police (sound familiar?) to arrest a "black homeless man, Leroy Summers," based solely on the idenitification of the second victim. A DNA test was performed three months later while Summers sat in a jail cell unable to post his $150,000 bail. The results excluded him as the perpetrator and led police to the real rapist. Citing a July 12, 2000, *News & Observer* article, the Durham-in-Wonderland blog quoted the prosecutor's comment after the DNA results came back negative: "Results of DNA evidence exclude the defendant as perpetrator of the crime." The prosecutor was Nifong!

3

BENCHED

Still determined to pin the crime on the lacrosse players, Nifong scheduled yet one more photo identification session. This time he was intent on making sure that Mangum couldn't help but identify her alleged attackers. On March 31, 2006, he met with Gottlieb and Himan to discuss using the "mug shot type photos" taken of the forty-six lacrosse team members pursuant to the NTO. They agreed to have Mangum simply look at each one of the photos to "see if she recalled seeing the individuals at the party."

A few days later, on April 3, 2006, Bob Ekstrand's investigator went to interview the Kroger security guard, Angel Altmon, an African American mother of five from West Virginia. At that point, neither the D.A.'s office nor the police had interviewed her. Altmon was the first woman that Mangum came into contact with besides Roberts after leaving the lacrosse party. During the interview, the investigator asked Altmon, "Is there any way this woman was sexually assaulted?" Her response was, "Ain't no way." Altmon was also asked if there was any mention on March 14 from either Mangum or Roberts of an assault or a rape. She said there wasn't and added that Mangum didn't act the way that Altmon would have expected someone to behave shortly after they had been assaulted or raped. Altmon also stated that Roberts told her she was driving down the street and heard people yelling racial slurs at a woman she had never met and that out of sympathy, she picked her up and brought her to Kroger's parking lot. It's odd that Roberts felt the need to continue with that lie. But that lie led the police straight to the boys. After leaving Durham Access, Mangum was transported to Duke University Hospital, and the police pieced together where she had been that night. A very scant audio of dispatch chatter was released where one officer was calling to the other saying that Mangum was with a girl in the Kroger parking lot. So they tied Mangum back to Kroger and to Roberts's statement that she had picked Mangum up at 610 North Buchanan, and it snowballed from there, one contradiction after another.

Mangum still hadn't identified her alleged attackers. Rather than performing a lineup or photo array as required by law, Mangum was brought to the Durham Police Department on April 4, 2006, for a "PowerPoint Identification." Sgt. Gottlieb sat down with her and told her, "We [are] going to sit in the far side of the room at the desk and look at people we [have] reason to believe attended the party." He also told her that it was "'important' for her to say whether she recalled 'seeing any of the persons to be shown and to describe what they were doing.'" Mangum proceeded to view the photos, and this time she identified four lacrosse players as her alleged attackers. This was how she pinpointed the boys:

> Picture #4—Matt Wilson: "He looked like Brett, but I'm not sure . . . One of the guys who assaulted me";
>
> Picture #5—David Evans: "He looks like one of the guys who assaulted me sort [of]. . . . He looks like him without the moustache . . . About 90%";
>
> Picture #7—Reade Seligmann: "He looks like one of the guys who assaulted me . . . 100% . . . He was the one that was standing in front of me . . . um . . . that made me perform oral sex on him";

Picture #40—Collin Finnerty: "He is the guy who assaulted
me. . . . He put his penis in my anus and my
vagina. . . . The second one . . . 100%."

Mangum also identified Brad Ross, Picture #9, as having attended the
party, "standing outside talking to the other dancer," but it was confirmed that he was not there that night; and Chris Loftus, Picture #26,
as being "in the living room . . . sitting down . . . I meant the master
bedroom," but it was also confirmed that he had left with his girlfriend and used his keycard to enter his dorm before the strippers had
even arrived at the party. Mangum also did not recognize three of the
people she had previously identified on March 16 and she claimed to
recognize eleven individuals that she did not recognize on March 16
or March 21. Additionally, during the March 16 session, Mangum recognized, after some hesitation, Adam Langley, Picture #11, as having
been at the party. She identified him again on April 4, saying that he
was in the master bedroom drinking. However, Langley was not
present at the party that night. Further, Mangum identified Tony
McDevitt, Picture #24, "as the person who made the comment
about the broomstick," yet prosecutors already knew that it was
Peter Lamade, Picture #20, who had made it. But Mangum identified
Lamade as "sitting in the kitchen . . . Um, making a drink."

This last identification session left a lot of unanswered questions,
as had all of the information obtained from Mangum. She had con-
tradicted herself once again, and even worse, the identification process
had been carried out in a manner that was clearly in violation of the
Durham Police Department's "General Order 4077," which sets forth
the procedures by which photo arrays must be performed and
which "was designed to prevent the conviction of innocent persons
and reduce the chance of mistaken identification." The identification procedures were also out of line with recommendations

made by the Actual Innocence Commission as endorsed by the North Carolina Criminal Justice Education and Training Standards Commission.

One glaring violation of the above procedures was the fact that the supervising investigator, Gottlieb, should not have been present during the identification sessions. An "independent administrator" is required in order to keep the process from having any appearance of bias. Further, as mentioned earlier, "fillers" are required, meaning that there should have been at least five pictures of random non-suspects for every one picture of a suspect put into the photo arrays. Additionally, if a case involves more than one suspect, all of their pictures can be used in a photo array, but there must still be five fillers for every suspect. Witnesses should also be instructed that the suspects *may or may not* be included in the photo array, rather than being told that all of the pictures are of people who might be suspects. Additionally, officials should not pressure a witness to make an identification, neither should they tell her that *"it is important"* to make such an ID. In summary, there were no independent administrators, no verbal safeguards, and no fillers used in this identification session. Mangum was given only pictures of lacrosse players to look at and was told to pick among them. This scenario simply stacked the deck against the boys. She couldn't make a wrong choice since the objective was to ensure that she would pick lacrosse players. Of course, it was not until Mangum was told that the photos she was viewing contained individuals whom police believed were at the party—and she therefore could not miss—that she identified anyone as an "attacker."

On the same day as the PowerPoint identification, April 4, 2006, Durham attorney Bill Thomas, who represents one of the lacrosse team captains, met with Nifong to discuss the case. At that time, Nifong was running in the primary for District Attorney of Durham, as mentioned earlier, a position he had originally been appointed to by North Carolina Governor Michael Easley when D.A. Jim Hardin was appointed to the Superior Court bench. Bill had been getting word from the courthouse that indictments were coming, so he tried to convince Nifong to slow down and not make any quick decisions to bring charges yet. At the very least, Bill suggested that Nifong should wait until after the election before indicting anyone to avoid the impression that his decision was politically motivated. Nifong's response was to show Bill the door.

On Wednesday, April 5, 2006, to everyone's surprise, the university announced that lacrosse coach Mike Pressler had "resigned." His sudden "decision" to leave the team left some people wondering whether he had actually been forced to quit. The circumstances surrounding Pressler's departure will be discussed at length in chapter 4.

On April 10, 2006, Dr. Brian Meehan, president and director of DSI, the second lab to test the lacrosse case DNA, met with Nifong and informed him that DSI had completed some of the Y-STR chromosome DNA tests, and this time DNA was found. However, none of it could be attributed to any of the lacrosse players. To the contrary, the specimens were determined to belong to multiple males, none of whom had anything to do with the lacrosse team or their party. Based on those findings, all of the lacrosse players should have been ruled out as suspects according to what Nifong's office had represented in its application for the NTO. But that did not happen. The potentially exculpatory test results were not released to defense attorneys. (Exculpatory evidence is information that may help to prove a defendant's innocence.)

According to Bob Ekstrand:

[T]he case, insofar as it ever was a case, ended on April 10, 2006. That was the day the SBI lab report was released to us, showing no match between any team member and genetic material found in the rape kit. It was also the day, unbeknownst to us, that Meehan told Nifong that his Y-STR testing—the most sensitive testing available—revealed multiple sources of male genetic material in [Mangum's] rape kit, [and] that each one of the forty-six members of the Duke Men's Lacrosse Team was conclusively excluded as a possible match to any of that male genetic material with a 100% degree of scientific certainty. Because Nifong and Meehan agreed to exclude those rudimentary facts from Meehan's report of the Y-STR testing, the case was quietly transformed into a cruel charade that lives on today. Because they refused to tell us what they knew to a 100% degree of scientific certainty, three demonstrably innocent boys were indicted for horrific crimes.

On Tuesday, April 11, 2006, Nifong sat on a panel at North Carolina Central University (NCCU), a historically black institution where Mangum was registered to attend classes. Still determined to move forward with his case against the lacrosse players, Nifong stated that even though no DNA had been found to connect the lacrosse players to the alleged rape, he was going to keep the case alive. While standing by his claims that Mangum was raped at the team party, Nifong said that "DNA results can often be helpful, but . . . I've been doing this for a long time, and for most of the years . . . we didn't have DNA. We had to deal with sexual assault cases the good old-fashioned way. Witnesses got on the stand and told what happened to them."

I was floored when I heard about Nifong's remark. While a believable witness can sometimes overcome the lack of any other evidence, that was not the case here. First, we do have the results from DNA tests that show absolutely no trace of any of the suspects on or in any part of the accuser. This is a huge hurdle that would be very difficult for the prosecution to overcome at trial without DNA testing to prove otherwise. I cannot imagine that any judge or jury could look at the facts of this case, hear a woman claim to have been brutally gang raped, beaten, and strangled by three guys who did not use condoms, and believe that they were guilty of the crime when not one drop of their DNA was found anywhere on the alleged victim.

However, on the highly unlikely chance that condoms had been used, let's look at the situation realistically. A rape exam is something that is performed very meticulously. I can't vouch for how it is done in North Carolina, but I would imagine that the SANE nurses around the United States are trained in a fairly consistent manner.

It is my understanding that a rape exam is performed this way: The victim gives a detailed history of the events of her assault. She or he is brought into an examination room where she/he stands on a sheet and removes all clothing. Everything is bagged and marked. She/he is examined from head to foot, and internally if penetration occurred. A rape kit is also used to collect physical evidence. Samples of a victim's hair, including pubic hair, are taken and put into special containers for testing. Scrapings are done on any type of dry liquids that appear to be on her/his skin, and those are also preserved for testing purposes. A special light is used to detect substances not seen under ordinary lighting. For a woman, if penetration occurred, a vaginal exam is performed manually, as well as with a spectrum. A machine is used with a screen similar to an ultrasound device. An instrument is inserted into the vagina and the SANE nurse can view on the screen whatever the instrument locates inside of the victim to see if there is anything that needs to be documented, photographed, swabbed, treated, or collected, i.e. swelling, bruising, bleeding, or foreign materials. An exam of the rectum is also performed if penetration occurred there. Swabs are taken of the victim's mouth, vagina, and rectum, if relevant. All bruises on the victim are photographed. Everything is then clearly marked for evidentiary purposes and sent to a lab for testing. If so much as a hair is on the victim or her/his clothing, it will be detected.

I explain these details in order to show just how unlikely it is for any of the "Duke Three," as Evans, Finnerty, and Seligmann were now collectively referred to, to have committed the crimes for which they are accused without having left a trace of DNA behind. Imagine, if you will, three young men who have been drinking and have lost their senses to the point where they rape a woman they hired to perform a dance. Then picture this: Mangum's claim is that the boys jostled her around into different positions while they beat her, kicked her, strangled her, sodomized her, took turns penetrating her orally, anally, and vaginally, and ejaculated in her mouth while she fought back so desperately that she was bruised and cut and some of her artificial nails were ripped off. Without taking a shower or washing, changing her clothes, brushing her teeth, or drinking or eating anything, she was taken to the hospital where she had a SANE exam. Can you now imagine that those three young men allegedly did all or even any of that to Mangum and not one single hair, not one drop of their saliva, semen, or blood was found during the sophisticated DNA testing that was performed at two separate labs? The point is that even if a condom was used, with the type of attack that Mangum described, it is inconceivable that any of the lacrosse players could have done any of these things to her without leaving *some* DNA evidence on or in her that would implicate some or all of them.

In addition to the fact that the DNA results were negative, an enormous amount of evidence exists in favor of the lacrosse team, not to mention all of the evidence undermining Mangum's credibility. But Nifong persisted at the NCCU meeting, telling the audience of several hundred people that the case "was not going away." The second DNA report had come back the day before, and Nifong knew what the results were. Yet, he stated that he had just ordered a new set of tests that wouldn't be back until May, as though there was a possi-bility that another round of testing would somehow implicate the lacrosse team.

Bob Ekstrand commented that attendees of the NCCU meeting were furious with Nifong. He apparently went there to be their cham-pion, but his attitude of "I'm not going to quit this case even though there's no DNA" must have puzzled the audience. Bob said the crowd seemed annoyed. Comments such as the following were made:

> If this happened at Central and the young lady was from another school and another persuasion, the outcome would have been different. [The students] would have been in jail. And everybody can make the comment that they wouldn't be, but there's a lot of young men in jail right now that are waiting on DNA. . . . So I understand that you all are going to say that that's not the case, cause you all have to give us political answers.

Another person, obviously highly incensed, said,

> Why did the accused rapists get a chance to chill out at Duke University? I know people that go to jail for being accused of rape or accused of battery or accused basically of anything and in my neighborhood, the police are out there like in minutes; they're in handcuffs; they're taken to court . . . and I want to know, why were they not arrested?

Bob said that he understood why those people were so angry, because that has been their experience, and when the police or the D.A. points a finger at African Americans in that part of North Carolina and says, "I'm sure there's a rape," they're taken away because they don't have the resources to defend themselves. According to Bob, "What Nifong basically accomplished at NCCU was that he ensured that he could chew on this case for another month until he got through the primary." But he needed an arrest. The next day, Nifong wrote an ex parte motion requesting that Judge Stevens sign an order that would seal the indictments of Collin Finnerty and Reade Seligmann.

On April 14, Durham attorney Bill Thomas tried once again to meet with Nifong. This time he brought along Butch Williams and Wade Smith, two other prominent attorneys who also represented team members. Their goal was to convince Nifong not to indict any of the boys, thereby preventing the lacrosse players from having to endure an unnecessary ordeal. According to Bill, "Wade Smith is a lawyer who is loved by every judge and every other lawyer; he's a scholar, and a wonderful person." Bill described Butch Williams as "an African American lawyer; probably one of the best lawyers, well thought of in the State, just a prince of a guy."

By now, the three attorneys were fully aware of Bob Ekstrand's timeline and the corroborating evidence, and they knew that Nifong's case was filled with holes. Bill said that the three of them tried to have a dialogue with Nifong. They offered to open up their files to show him the timeline and the photographs of the scene as well as other evidence, and to explain that Mangum's story didn't make sense when compared to the hard evidence that they had. The attorneys asked Nifong not to indict, and told him that they were willing to share their defense with him so he could consider it prior to an indictment. Bill commented to me that he didn't think they could have met more resistance. He added, "I thought having the three of us there, Nifong would receive us knowing that we were coming to share the truth. I remember all of us looking at each other just as we were getting ready to leave, wondering if we could say anything that would change his mind, but there was nothing to say. The train was going and it wasn't going to stop. Nifong thanked us for our time and showed us the door."

Bob Ekstrand had discussed his timeline with the three attorneys prior to their meeting with Nifong. The plan was simple and seemed reasonable. The three attorneys were going as a group of emissaries who Nifong might trust and thus be willing to consider what they had to say. They hoped that they could sit down with the D.A. and suggest to him that indicting someone right now would be a big mistake, and they could at least get him to consider more carefully what he was about to do. According to Bob, the three men basically said to Nifong, "You have no evidence to support an indictment and to the extent that you think you do, you really have to look at what we have. We don't want you to tell us what you have. This is not an exchange that we're proposing. What we are proposing to you is a meeting where we will show you the evidence in this case that we believe is compelling proof of innocence."

Nifong's response was, "You haven't interviewed this witness, but I have and she's going to be a good witness and you and I know that that's all it takes."

Reade Seligmann's attorney, the late J. Kirk Osborn, also attempted to meet with Nifong in the hopes that he could convince him through a showing of documented exculpatory evidence to drop the charges. Osborn wasn't even invited into the D.A.'s private office for a meeting. Nifong sent someone out to tell him that he had seen Osborn on television talking about his client's innocence, so there was nothing for the men to discuss.

It became clear that Nifong would not let this case go because it had apparently become a vehicle for his election and, as Bob so aptly put it, "He was going to ride these boys into office." Bob and I could not find any other explanation for why a prosecutor would not accept an unconditional offer to see all of the defendant's evidence in a case. There is no down side to seeing an opponent's evidence. The evidence could either be harmful to a case or it could be helpful. Either way, any lawyer would want to have this information. If such disclosure *is* harmful to a case, an attorney needs to be aware of it ahead of time in order to have an opportunity prior to trial to figure out how to rebut it or otherwise deal with it. If it is helpful, an attorney will be able to use it to assist his or her own case. But Nifong wasn't interested. He had his mind made up, and his next move revealed how far he was willing to push the case.

On April 17, Nifong sought indictments against two of the Duke lacrosse players, Collin Finnerty and Reade Seligmann. After rejecting the offers of evidence from the defense attorneys who contended that their clients had alibis or otherwise did not commit the crime and would take polygraphs to prove it, and in spite of DSI's DNA results absolving all of the lacrosse players of rape, as well as Nifong's office's prior representation in the application for the NTO that the "DNA evidence requested will immediately rule out any innocent persons," Nifong indicted Collin Finnerty and Reade Seligmann for first-degree rape, first-degree sex offense, and kidnapping.

It could have been even worse for the boys. Bob told me that the arrests had been arranged in a way that would have enabled police to apprehend the boys while in class. Unbeknownst to them, after their indictment, there was to be a perp walk across the Duke quad with the national media in tow. Bob said that the other attorneys were able to convince Judge Stevens not to permit the perp walk to happen. They asked the judge to allow the boys to turn themselves in on the following Tuesday morning and he agreed.

Unbelievable! Nifong was going to have these kids arrested in class, right in front of the other students, and paraded across campus in front of the potbangers, reporters, and cameras from countless media sources, and the whole world. The man was willing to sacrifice these boys in order to further his own career. Clearly, if that was his plan, he has no conscience. He knew he had no case, and he just didn't seem to care.

On Tuesday, April 18, 2006, twenty-year-olds Collin Finnerty and Reade Seligmann turned themselves in to the authorities. After they were booked, they each posted bond in the amount of $400,000 and were released. The excessive amount of the bond was unprecedented under the circumstances. The following day, Finnerty and Seligmann received more disturbing news. They were being suspended from Duke University and sent home, a devastating disruption of everything they had worked toward up until that moment in their lives.

Within a few days of the indictments, additional testing at DSI on another piece of evidence from the rape kit revealed DNA characteristics from multiple males, none of whom were lacrosse team members. By this time, the investigation was in full swing, and the community was pushing for more arrests.

On April 19, 2006, J. Kirk Osborn, counsel for Reade Seligmann, served Nifong with a request for discovery material, including witness statements, the results of any tests, all DNA analysis, and any exculpatory information.

The next day, April 20, 2006, Duke University President Richard Brodhead was quoted by WRAL-TV commenting to the Durham Chamber of Commerce that "If our students did what is alleged, it is appalling to the worst degree If they didn't do it, whatever they did is bad enough." In my opinion, that was just another example of Brodhead's lack of support for his students. What is particularly disturbing about this is that defense attorneys had already offered Brodhead and his administrators more than sufficient evidence to discredit the allegations that had been made against the boys. But they refused to review it. In addition, the three players who lived in the house had previously met with Brodhead face-to-face, looked him in the eye, and told him in no uncertain terms that the criminal allegations against the players were totally false. Thus, when Brodhead made that comment, it was with a blatant disregard for the truth, and his statement left the boys open to harsh ridicule and condemnation even though they had not committed the crimes for which they had been charged.

On April 21, 2006, Dr. Brian Meehan, the head of DSI, met with Nifong, Gottlieb, and Himan and informed them of the latest DNA test results. Nifong made a decision that would eventually come back to haunt him. He instructed Meehan to only include in the final report "positive" test results between the lacrosse players and Mangum, meaning that the exculpatory evidence, the results showing that DNA from several other men had been found in Mangum, would be excluded from the report. Although he was violating DSI's own policy that "results of every test" must be included in every report, Dr. Meehan agreed. This "conspiracy of silence" allowed Nifong to continue moving full speed ahead to prosecute the lacrosse players while knowing that the evidence, or lack thereof, was clearly in their favor.

On May 1, 2006, attorneys for Reade Seligmann filed a motion to suppress non-testimonial photographs. The purpose of the motion was to prevent the photo lineup from being used as evidence against Seligmann. The basis for the motion was that the non-testimonial order that was used to obtain the samples of DNA and pictures of the lacrosse players was "unconstitutional and unlawful." In essence, the defense attorneys asserted that the government did not have the necessary probable cause to obtain the NTO in the first place, rendering any evidence that was born from it (in legal terms) "fruit of the poisonous tree," in other words, invalid. Putting it plainly, since the application for the NTO contained inaccurate information, any evidence obtained from its enforcement should not be used against the defendant. Thus, the NTO procedure itself, the identification of the suspects, and any in-court identification of the suspects should be suppressed (disregarded) because the taking of the photographs and DNA samples pursuant to the NTO was illegal and unconstitutional.

Here is the reasoning behind the motion. On March 23, 2006, Assistant District Attorney David Saacks applied for the NTO using Investigator Himan's affidavit to support it. The affidavit stated that, according to Mangum, three men, "Adam, Brett, and Matt," attacked her. However, there were no descriptions of her alleged attackers in the affidavit. Additionally, according to the defense motion, the Durham Police Department already possessed a substantial amount of evidence by which Mangum's claims of sexual assault could have been discredited, but Himan excluded that information from his affidavit. The motion also raised the issue that there was no explanation of why the forty-six lacrosse team members were named in the affidavit aside from the fact that the three team captains who resided at 610 North Buchanan Boulevard stated that lacrosse team members had attended the party. In particular, Himan's affidavit indicated that everyone on the list, *except for the last five*, was named by the three residents of 610 North Buchanan, Evans, Flannery, and Zash, as having been present at the party. Strangely, Reade Seligmann's name was #42 on the list of 46. Therefore, using Himan's information, Seligmann should not even have been on the NTO's list. Further, and even more interesting, is that, as mentioned earlier, David Evans told investigators on March 16, 2006, that there were "two or three fraternity guys" at the party and one of them "was named Blake." Yet their names were not included in the NTO, and their pictures were not contained in any of the photo arrays that Mangum was shown to identify her alleged assailants.

Here is my take on why those two or three people were not included. We now know that one of the most important facts that was constantly being publicized during the investigation was incorrect:

that it was the whole team and nothing but the team that was at the lacrosse party on March 13, 2006. However, that incorrect notion made possible the theory that there was particularized suspicion for each member of the group of forty-six lacrosse players. As Bob Ekstrand noted, "As soon as you pierce that perfect theory with two or three non-lacrosse players being present and the fact that the boys who gave statements said that a number of lacrosse players were not there and that they made a rough guess as to how many *were* there," you lose the ability to obtain an NTO covering the entire lacrosse team. While it is unclear whether A.D.A. David Saacks was aware of those facts when he applied for the NTO, Himan surely was.

So, what does this really mean? In order to obtain the NTO that ordered the entire lacrosse team to submit to photographs and DNA testing, the government had to demonstrate to the judge that "there is probable cause to believe that a felony had been committed, [that] there are reasonable grounds to suspect that the person named or described in the affidavit committed the offense, and that the results of the specific non-testimonial identification procedures will be of material aid in determining whether the person named in the affi-davit committed the offense." In other words, since the affidavit merely suggested that three men out of a group of forty-six may have committed the crimes alleged by Mangum, the defense motion is asserting that "the non-testimonial order violated the Fourth, Fifth, Sixth, and Fourteenth Amendments to the United States Constitution and Article I, Sections 19 and 20 of the North Carolina Constitution, in that there was no individualized suspicion that the defendant com-mitted the crimes" alleged by Mangum. Thus, based on what Himan wrote in the supporting affidavit and the evidence on which he based his statements, there was not enough information to warrant order-ing Seligmann or, in fact, any or all of the forty-six young men to sub-mit to DNA testing or having their pictures taken.

By May 12, 2006, all of the DNA tests were completed, and Nifong received his report. The main items noted involved DNA on two fingernails that were "at least partially consistent with the DNA profile of two unindicted lacrosse players and a sperm fraction from the vaginal swab that was consistent with the DNA profile of the alleged victim's boyfriend." Nothing was mentioned in the report about the multiple male DNA specimens that were detected or the fact that tests had been performed on items that were identified as having "potentially exculpatory evidence." Pursuant to the discovery request made on April 19, 2006, Nifong turned the report over to the defense counsel for Finnerty and Seligmann and also gave it to attorneys for David Evans with no mention of the omitted test results or the potentially exculpatory evidence.

Three days later, on May 15, 2006, the day after twenty-three-year-old David Evans graduated from Duke, he was indicted for first-degree rape, first-degree sex offense, and kidnapping. Like his two indicted teammates, Evans was booked and released on a $400,000 bond.

Prior to turning himself in, Evans spoke to the media, making him the first of the "Duke Three" to publicly respond to the allegations. Evans stood in front of countless television cameras and reporters, looked everyone squarely in the eye, and made a very compelling statement.

> I want to thank you all for letting me speak to you today. My name is Dave Evans and I'm a captain of the Duke University men's lacrosse team. I have to say that I am very relieved to be the person to speak out on behalf of my family and my team and let you know how we feel. First I want to say that I am absolutely innocent of all of the charges brought against me today, that Reade Seligmann and Collin Finnerty are also innocent of all the charges that were brought against them.

These allegations are lies, fabricated, and they will be proven wrong.

If I can go back to two months ago when the police first came to my home, I fully cooperated and I've continued to try to cooperate with them. When they entered in and started to read the search warrant, my roommates and I helped them find evidence for almost an hour and told them that if they had any questions we would gladly answer them to show that nothing happened that night. After that, I went down to the police station and gave an uncounseled statement because I knew that I had done nothing wrong and did not feel that I needed an attorney. After going through photos of my team-mates and identifying who was there, I then submitted, perfectly willingly, DNA samples to the police. I then turned over my e-mail account, my AIM account, any kind of information that they could have to show that I had not communicated in any way that anything had happened because it did not happen. After that, I asked to take a polygraph which was refused by the Durham Police Department.

Over the past several weeks, I have repeatedly, through my lawyer, tried to contact the District Attorney. All of my attempts have been denied. I have tried to provide him with exculpatory evidence showing that this could not have happened. Those attempts have been denied. And as a result of his apparent lack of interest in my story, the true story, and any evidence proving that my story is correct, I asked my lawyer to give me a poly-graph. I took that polygraph, and it was administered by a for-mer FBI top polygrapher with over twenty-eight years of experience. He's done several hundreds of sexual cases and I passed it absolutely. And I passed that polygraph for the same reason that I will be acquitted of all these charges, because I have done nothing wrong and I am telling the truth and I have told the truth from day one.

I'd like to say thank you to my friends and family, my coach, and members of the community who have stood by us through everything from the initial weeks to now. Their support has given me the strength to come through this, but the thing that gives me the most strength is knowing that I have the truth behind me and it will not faze me.

If I can close, I've always taken pride in my name. I take pride in my name today and I'll gladly stand up to anything that comes against me. I've never had my character questioned before. Anyone who has met me knows that this didn't happen. I appreciate your support. As for my teammates, I love you all. The honor of being voted captain of all of you, the forty-six best guys you could meet . . .

Evans continued, though his voice began filling with emotion,

. . . it's been the best honor of my life. If I can clear things up and say this one more time, I am innocent. Reade Seligmann is innocent. Collin Finnerty is innocent. Every member of the Duke University lacrosse team is innocent. You have all been told some fantastic lies and I look forward to watching them unravel in the weeks to come as they already have in weeks passed and the truth will come out. Thank you for your time.

I had taken some time off that week, and my wife and I went to the beach at Sandestin, Florida, for a few days. We happened to be in our hotel room and turned on the TV when they telecast Evans's live statement. As I watched him speak, I told my wife, Barbara, that I thought he was outstanding. I just stopped what I was doing and listened to him, and I said right then and there, "Wow, this is amazing. That kid is absolutely telling the truth."

Based on what I knew prior to Evans's statement, I was already inclined to believe that the boys were innocent of the allegations against them, and this only confirmed what my instincts had been telling me. After so many years of experience trying lawsuits, you develop a certain sense about people's credibility when they are testifying or even just speaking. As I watched Evans, I could clearly tell from looking at his demeanor and hearing what he had to say and the manner in which he said it that he was not guilty of the horrendous crimes with which he and his teammates were charged. Watching this told me a great deal about this young man. I was very impressed. What he said was so powerful, and how he said it was so convincing, that he had to be telling the truth. For a young man at his age and under those circumstances to be able to stand there and be so strong, articulate, and calm is just amazing. And to be able to look right in the eyes of the hordes of those who may be thinking he's guilty, to do that, he had be telling the truth.

Moreover, there is another significant thought that occurred to me as a lawyer. This young man had just been indicted of some very serious crimes that could conceivably put him away for most of his life if convicted, and he was being represented by some very capable lawyers who were standing right there behind him as he spoke to the masses. These are good lawyers who would never have allowed him to do this, they would never take this risk, unless they had fully investigated the case and were absolutely positive that he and the other boys were innocent of the charges.

Since Evans had graduated, suspension in his case was not an issue. Finnerty and Seligmann, were not so lucky. After being banned from school grounds by the Duke administration, the two younger lacrosse players left the hostile and unsupportive environment for home. They had already endured the accusations, the threats, the demonstrations, the hatred, the fear, and the isolation. Now it was time for them to retreat to safety and let the wheels of justice turn. But justice was a far cry from what they were about to get in Durham, where Nifong held the reins of injustice so tightly in his grip.

4

DUKED

Nifong wasn't the only one who would victimize the Dukies, although he may have been the fuel that fired up the others. President Brodhead had allowed the players to be suspended without taking the time to even view or consider the evidence that had been offered to him. He also failed to comprehend the implications of the undercurrent that was brewing on and around his campus. And he had been making comments that left people wondering exactly where he stood in regard to the lacrosse team. One such comment was made on April 5, 2006, to WRAL when Brodhead said that "the allegations have left Duke with a reputation of arrogant inconsiderateness, but [that] the majority of Duke students are well-behaved and good-hearted." While I can certainly appreciate Brodhead's concern for public relations for the school, I was disappointed that he appeared to be more concerned with what people thought of Duke than whether or not the boys were being treated fairly. This statement was puzzling to me. Was Brodhead sending out some sort of subliminal message that the students who were *not* well-behaved and good-hearted were the lacrosse team members?

On May 17, 2006, attorneys for Collin Finnerty served Nifong with discovery requests specifically asking him to turn over any and all DNA test results and reports. They also requested that any information that was discussed between Nifong and the DNA expert, Dr. Meehan, be memorialized (written down) and submitted. Nifong filed written responses to the discovery requests representing that "The

State is not aware of any additional material or information which may be exculpatory in nature with respect to the defendant[s]."

On May 18, 2006, Nifong furnished all three defense attorneys with discovery materials, including another copy of DSI's DNA report. However, there was "no underlying data or information concerning DSI's testing and analysis" or any indication that there was potentially exculpatory DNA evidence. In other words, he still did not give the defense attorneys the evidence that could help prove their clients' innocence. Further, Nifong did not provide the defense with any documentation of the conversations he had with Dr. Meehan in April and May 2006 in regard to the potentially exculpatory evidence. At a May 18, 2006, hearing, the court asked Nifong whether he had turned over all discovery materials to the defendants, and he responded, "I've turned over everything I have."

At the same time that Nifong was deceiving the court, the university's stance was equally unnerving; Brodhead's failure to stand by the accused and hold off on taking disciplinary action until more of the investigation had been revealed to him was inexcusable. At the very least, he could have used Professor Coleman's committee report to turn back the tide on those who were making the allegations into a widespread campus problem. Coleman's report contained many positive findings regarding the lacrosse team, including the fact that the lacrosse players were "academically and athletically responsible students," that their "academic performance was one of the best among all Duke athletic teams, that they are a cohesive, hard-working, disciplined, and respectful athletic team," and that they participated extensively in community service.

Rather than focus on these positive assessments from the committee that he had appointed to investigate these matters, on June 5, 2006, Brodhead issued a letter to the Duke community in which he added an addendum of negativity to the end of each favorable remark, as though to cancel it out. One glaring statement in his letter read as follows: "Though it did not confirm the worst allegations against this team, the Coleman Committee documented a history of irresponsible conduct that this university cannot allow to continue." With this statement, he clearly gave the impression that the lacrosse team was a major problem. My own sense is that Brodhead was merely trying to justify or rationalize his inappropriate decision to send the boys home. Hopefully, everyone reading those words was aware that, in truth, Brodhead's statement applied to behavior that is not highly unusual among college students at universities across the country, such as underage drinking and the desire to watch young women dance provocatively. While I am not condoning those actions, I am also not going to totally condemn a bunch of kids whose immature judgment led them to do things that they would have otherwise shunned given the life experience of ten or twenty years.

The biggest mistake that these kids made, in my opinion, was putting themselves in the position where something like this could happen to them. First, they hired total strangers to strip and dance for them. It should come as no surprise that women who are willing to do that for money at a party full of strangers might not be individuals of the highest moral character, and that they just might cause bad things to happen at the party. Second, the hosts served alcohol to students who were not yet legally old enough to drink. They were boys doing what college boys often do. And while this was not smart on their part since, at the very least, if discovered by the school, they would be subject to disciplinary measures, it by no means merited the manner in which they were treated.

Brodhead also wrote the following in his letter of June 5, 2006, cited earlier: "Whether or not the felony charges are upheld against the three indicted students, the fact is that members of the team engaged in irresponsible and dishonorable behavior on the evening of March

13, 2006, and those who were involved bear responsibility for their actions." I completely agree, but let's keep it in the proper perspective. The prospect of being sent to prison for the better part of the rest of their lives is an unreasonable consequence for underage drinking and hiring strippers to dance at a party.

Attorney Bill Thomas suggested to me that Brodhead really wasn't holding the reigns in the decision-making process when it came to the school's handling of the lacrosse case. According to him, many believe that Bob Steel, Chairman of the Board of Trustees at Duke University, and Under Secretary of the U.S. Treasury, has been the central figure in overseeing how the situation has been handled. If Bill's assessment is accurate, then Steel has apparently been displaying more interest in the negative public relations issues arising from this case than the constitutional rights of the boys on the lacrosse team.

Early on, Steel, the man assigned the responsibility of bringing Brodhead to Duke in the first place, made sure that nobody would get the impression that team members were actually enjoying life on the lacrosse field in the face of the rape allegations. Their practices had to end, and the team could no longer continue with its season for fear of giving the wrong impression. Steel made it known that he considered it a public relations nightmare to have team members portrayed in newspapers going about their normal routines. I can only wonder why he wasn't as concerned about the type of impression that his dual roles as government servant and Duke Board of Trustees Chairman emit. After all, considering all of the confidential financial information that Steel has access to in his new government position, it is questionable as to whether he is truly able to juggle the responsibility of being Under Secretary with his job of watching out for the best interests of Duke, a university that is not only the beneficiary of federal funds, but also has billions of dollars in investments. While I'm not trying to shift blame away from Brodhead, Steel holds a significant amount of leverage over him, and it's possible that he has been the driving force in calling the shots in the handling of the lacrosse case. However, it is difficult to assume, given Brodhead's past (which will soon be discussed at length), that he is not fully responsible for the decisions coming out of the administration.

During further research into the lacrosse case, I also had the privilege of interviewing Dr. Steven Baldwin, a Duke chemistry professor who has been at the school since 1970. After a few minutes with him, it was apparent to me that he was a professor who loved Duke and took great interest in his pupils. He began by discussing the boys' suspensions with me.

> What Duke claims, the reason that they suspended the two indicted players . . . was that it was a policy or a guideline. I think they justify the suspension not because [the boys] were a threat to the community, but that it wasn't clear how the community would react on campus. A sizeable group of people thought that these kids had done something really wrong and they had been indicted.

Baldwin said he wouldn't have suspended them. He explained his rationale to me. He said that because Duke is a private institution, they aren't under the same restrictions or tied to the same policies as a public institution that is responsible to the government and has no choice but to take action when the pressure is on them. A private school has the power to make its own policy decisions. Baldwin felt that Duke administrators had the ability to sit back and wait while the evidence was revealed, and more importantly, to stand up for the boys. But they didn't. He felt that "Brodhead should have come out and said right off the bat, 'These are our students and we're going to make sure they have all the advantages of the legal system as prescribed by the

Constitution and due process. We're behind them. If they're guilty and they need to deal with it, they will. But in the meantime, they're innocent.'" This is essentially the same position that Duke basketball coach Mike Krzyzewski, affectionately referred to by Dukies as "Coach K," endorsed in his public statement "that Duke would be so much better off if it had taken that position. It would have made so much more sense for all concerned."

Through my continuing investigation into the months following the lacrosse party allegations, I came to realize that Brodhead had made several other errors in judgment, possibly the worst being the firing, or forced resignation, of lacrosse coach Mike Pressler, a man who had spent sixteen seasons at Duke and had led the team to win three Atlantic Coast Conference (ACC) Championships. Even more notable, from an educational standpoint, is the fact that during Pressler's tenure at Duke, his players had a graduation rate of 100 percent. According to Eddie Falcone, Pressler's attorney, in an April 6, 2006, statement on behalf of Duke lacrosse coach Mike Pressler, which was posted on WRAL.com, the players were also "heavily involved in community service projects." Additionally, he said that during the past five years, 146 of Pressler's players were on the ACC Academic Honor Role, 74 more than the next closest school.

I have made several references to Pressler's "firing or forced resignation." The public perception is that he handed in his resignation on his own without any discussion. However, Baldwin told me otherwise. He said that after Pressler's resignation was announced, he (Baldwin) sent an e-mail to Brodhead asking for a meeting. They agreed to meet the week after graduation. Baldwin and Coach Pressler are good friends. Baldwin requested the meeting with Brodhead because he wanted the coach reinstated. At the time, it wasn't clear to him if Pressler had been fired or had resigned. So, at the meeting he came right out and asked Brodhead. Brodhead's response began with

"When I made the decision to fire Coach Pressler. . . ." Baldwin had his answer. Then he asked a follow-up question, "What's the logic here?" Brodhead answered, "I think that lacrosse will come back at Duke. I think we will reinstate it. But it can't ever be the same. It will be different. And the only way to make sure it's different is to have a new coach." Baldwin expressed his disagreement with Brodhead. "That doesn't make any sense at all," he countered, adding that "we can make it different by laying down ground rules that apply to all athletes; you can't tell me that there aren't other groups on campus, athletic and non-athletic groups that aren't doing things like drinking and having parties. This isn't a lacrosse issue. It's just focused on lacrosse right now." Brodhead ended the conversation with, "That was my decision and that's the way it's going to be. There's no possibility that Pressler will be reinstated." Baldwin called Brodhead's decision to fire Pressler a "rush to judgment." This wasn't the first time Brodhead had made a hasty decision that had long-term consequences for people under his charge.

A little research into Brodhead's history allowed me to put his handling of the lacrosse incident into the proper perspective. I discovered that in 1998, while Brodhead was a Dean at Yale University, there was an incident involving a young woman named Suzanne Jovin. She had been writing her senior thesis on a fellow named Osama Bin Laden under the direction of her essay advisor, political science lecturer James Van de Velde. On December 4, 1998, Jovin was found dead after having been stabbed seventeen times in what police labeled a crime of passion. Van de Velde was named one of many suspects. Brodhead, along with other Yale administrators, immediately agreed to cancel Van de Velde's classes. According to an interview with Van de Velde published in a February 5, 2004, article on Yaledailynews.com entitled "The Unusual Suspect," "on January 10, 1999, Brodhead left a message on Van de Velde's answering machine telling him to meet him at his office. Brodhead and [another administrator] were waiting for Van de Velde when he arrived. Van de Velde was quoted in the article as saying that '[Brodhead] began this strange soliloquy about the presumption of innocence. I can always tell when Dick is nervous because he kind of rambles.' At that point," the article continues, "Brodhead handed him a letter, telling him that he would not be teaching classes in the spring semester."

Brodhead's actions left no room for a presumption of innocence. Van de Velde was never charged with anything. In fact, Jovin had skin underneath her fingernails that wasn't DNA tested for two years, and when it was finally analyzed, the DNA didn't match Van de Velde's. The point is that there appears to be a pattern of rushing to judgment on Brodhead's part, firing the coach, canceling the season, suspending the students (as will be discussed shortly), and firing the faculty member.

Like Pressler, Van de Velde had a stellar reputation, having been a State Department expert on nuclear arms control, a White House appointee under former President George H. W. Bush, and Dean of Yale's Saybrook College. But according to a June 6, 2006, article in Nationalreviewonline.com entitled "Forget the Facts," Van De Velde was considered a "black sheep" at Yale. He "was the subject of personal jealousy and political animosity. Many faculty members—including Brodhead—looked askance at [Van de Velde's] desire to emphasize practical policymaking over theory. Some questioned, for example, [Van de Velde's] willingness to help Jovin write—in 1998—about the threat posed by Osama bin Laden to the U.S., to be unscholarly." The article also referred to Van de Velde as a "sacrificial lamb."

The Van de Velde incident wasn't the end of the story in regard to Brodhead's questionable administrative decision-making policies.

While visiting Duke, I was told of a young Yale University senior named Naomi Wolf who claimed that she had been sexually harassed by a well-respected Yale English Professor, Harold Bloom. I did some research and was able to find an article that Wolf wrote in the March 1, 2004, issue of *New York Magazine* entitled "The Silent Treatment" detailing what had happened to her in 1983 and the events that followed. She hadn't told anyone at the time of the incident, but it tormented her for many years until she finally decided to discuss it with university officials. She called Yale, and after receiving no response from others, she contacted Brodhead, then a dean at Yale, and requested a meeting. She said that Brodhead "seemed to know who [she] was talking about" and "implied the man in question was not well." Wolf explained to Brodhead that she was not interested in suing either Yale or Harold Bloom; she also assured him that she wanted to keep the whole matter private. She was just trying to make sure that "Yale's grievance procedures are . . . strong." Brodhead told her that he would get back to her. He never did. Wolf eventually called someone else who referred the matter back to Brodhead. Again, she didn't hear from him. Through the course of her own investigation, Wolf came to realize that this was the type of issue that the university, Brodhead included, often turned a blind eye to. To support her contention, she cited a 1996 article in the *Yale Daily News*, which "reported that the Grievance Board had found that an assistant math professor had consensual sex with a freshman whom he was grading." The board's recommendation was to keep the professor from teaching undergraduates during that semester. Brodhead went against the decision, telling the Yale paper that he "didn't think it would be possible to find a replacement that quickly." According to Wolf, "the paper also reported that the head of the math department said no one had ever called to ask if there was someone else to teach the course."

Over one month prior to writing her article, Wolf had been informed that Yale had a "seemingly exemplary description of its grievance procedure," and she requested a copy of it from Brodhead. He hadn't sent it as of her article's publication.

I found it interesting that certain people were allowed to stay under the radar on Brodhead's watch, while others were hung out to dry. That practice seems to have followed Brodhead to Duke. Coach Pressler's "firing" had come after Durham police unsealed a warrant that revealed details of the alleged incident at the lacrosse house. Included in the warrant was an e-mail from lacrosse player Ryan McFadyen. Apparently, a confidential source turned the e-mail over to Sgt. Gottlieb. The contents of the e-mail were disclosed in the probable cause affidavit attached to the application for a search warrant of McFadyen's dorm room and car. The e-mail had been sent out on the morning of March 14, 2006, at 1:58 a.m., unbeknownst to any of the lacrosse players, shortly after Mangum had been brought to the Duke University Hospital emergency room. It read exactly as follows:

> To whom it may concern:
> Tomorrow night, after tonights show, ive decided to have some strippers over to edens 2c. all are welcome. However there will be no nudity. I plan on killing the bitches as soon as the walk in and proceding to cut their skin off while cumming in my duke issue spandex..all in besides arch and tack please respond.
> 41

The number 41 is McFadyen's jersey number. Several sources have told me that McFadyen is known as a joker, someone who pulls the kinds of stunts you would expect from a college kid. Those close to him recognized the e-mail as something taken out of a scene from *American Psycho,* a novel by Bret Easton Ellis that was turned into a movie and that sources told me has been part of the curriculum of at least three psychology classes at Duke as an example of current pop culture. I've also been told that eventually the e-mail was understood as nothing more than a prank gone wrong. As punishment for the e-mail, McFadyen was given an interim suspension from school after the Vice President for Student Affairs, Larry Moneta, decided that he posed a risk to himself or others. The significance of this follows. In an April 5, 2006, article in www.newsobserver.com, President Brodhead was quoted as saying that "in situations where a threat to the safety of an individual or members of the university community exists, Vice President Moneta typically executes an interim suspension." If what Brodhead said is true, then I can only wonder how he would explain Moneta's handling of the following incident.

As unnerving as McFadyen's e-mail was, it didn't compare to the one that Coach Pressler received shortly thereafter. Apparently, the coach had been receiving numerous harassing e-mails in regard to the lacrosse incident. One such e-mail came from Duke student Chauncy Narty. Several sources have confirmed that the e-mail was sent on March 27, 2006, at 2:01 p.m. The e-mail's subject read, "WHAT IF JANET LYNN WERE NEXT???" Janet is Coach Pressler's daughter's name. I was told that Pressler brought the e-mail to Vice President Moneta, and it was traced to Narty, an African American student. After what is assumed to have been an investigation into the matter, Pressler was told that the e-mail was not regarded as a threat. Thus, no action was taken, not in the form of punishment, that is. So, McFadyen was suspended for sending an e-mail out to his friends as a joke, while Narty sent an e-mail that contained at least an implied threat to the lacrosse coach and was simply told not to do it again.

Here's the interesting twist in regard to the e-mail situation. Within a couple of weeks of Mangum's lacrosse allegations, Brodhead formed five committees to investigate the issues that arose out of it. One such committee was the Campus Cultural Initiative Steering Committee, and it was headed up by Larry Moneta and Vice Provost for Undergraduate Education and Dean of Trinity College Robert

Thompson. Brodhead stated, "The task of the Initiative is to evaluate and suggest improvements in the ways Duke educates students in the values of personal responsibility, consideration for others, and mutual respect in the face of difference and disagreement." You may be wondering what this has to do with the e-mail. This information is relevant because when you look at the responsibilities of the Committee, and you see that Moneta is at its helm, and then you learn that one of his appointees to this Committee is Narty, the student who sent the allegedly threatening e-mail out to Pressler, you have to question what is really going on in the administrative offices of Duke University.

5

THE TAIL WAGS THE DOG

At this point it was clear that the Duke administration had, for the most part, apparently abandoned the lacrosse team. At a time when the boys were at their lowest, when the evils of hate, vengeance, and racism were banging on their doors, those who had the boys' lives in their charge did not stand guard to protect them. Team members were treated like criminals, guilty until proven innocent.

At the very least, we should expect that when we send our children off to college they will be in the care of responsible administrators who will take on the role of overseer. Although those administrators could never replace us as parents, it is my belief that they should, in many respects, treat their students like their own kids. They should be willing to support them and stand by them during the trying times that many college kids face. And on those occasions that are not fore-seeable, such as when patently false accusations are made and a dis-trict attorney trounces on the lives of not only the kids but their families and their school for his own personal gain, university admini-strators have an obligation to take charge of the situation and let their students know that they will do everything in their power to see that their constitutional rights are protected. Otherwise, those to whom we have entrusted our children will have failed us.

Members of the lacrosse team, most notably Evans, Finnerty, and Seligmann, were, in fact, abandoned. And we, as parents, do not aban-don our children. There may be times when we are not as proud of them as we would hope, but we do not turn our backs on them. There

91

may be moments when we may lie awake staring into the darkness wondering where we went wrong, but we do not abandon our kids. We stand by them while seeking the truth. We give them the benefit of the doubt, and even if they have faltered, we prop them up until they no longer need our support. We hope that they learn lessons from the difficult moments in their lives, and we recognize that it is moments such as those that will help build their character and strengthen and mold them into the type of adults that we all wish our children to become.

The Duke administration did not give the boys the benefit of the doubt. They stood back and watched from the sidelines while Nifong dragged them through the mud. The administrators refused to protect them, not even truly acknowledging the possibility that they were innocent and that Nifong was railroading them straight into his political victory. Forty-seven lacrosse players were punished in the end. Their season was ripped away from them. Their coach was fired. Forty-six of them were forced to give DNA samples and have mug shots taken. They were harassed and ridiculed, and the administration wouldn't even allow them to have excused absences when serious threats were being made against their lives. Instead, the boys were told to take it up with their professors, some of whom were even criticizing them in front of their classmates and handing them failing grades simply because they were members of the lacrosse team. Worst of all, faculty members publicly chastised them for what they automatically assumed was their "racist" and "sexist" behavior.

I believe that a gang rape did occur at Duke University, and it did begin on the night of March 13, 2006. But it is figurative in nature, and, to date, it hasn't ended. The victims of that vicious attack are the boys who were indicted, Evans, Finnerty, and Seligmann, their forty-four teammates, their coach, and their families. This atrocity took place in no small part because people like Richard Brodhead caved in to the demands of the loudest and crudest members of his faculty, the rush to judgment brought on by the onslaught of extreme political correctness and the lack of courage to stand up for the rights of these young men.

One wheel on the campus bandwagon for conviction was the "Group of 88," also known as the "Duke 88," a menagerie of professors from mainly the social sciences who used the lacrosse case as their soapbox to emphasize the need for change in a system they claim is pervaded by sexual harassment and racial discrimination. In April 2006, they put a full-page ad in the school newspaper, *The Chronicle*, and had it posted (subsequently removed) on Duke's African-American Studies Web site letting everyone know that they were "listening." Listing a handful of comments from unnamed students allegedly concerned about racism and sexism on campus, members of the Group of 88 wrote that they were "turning up the volume in a moment when some of the most vulnerable among us are being asked to quiet down while we wait. To the students speaking individually and to the protestors making collective noise, thank you for not waiting and for making yourselves heard."

I couldn't help wondering exactly to whom they were aiming their gratitude. A minute of reflection allowed me to see their ad for what it truly was, a call to action, an incitement to act first and think later. It was a thank-you note to people like the potbangers and the drummers and those who screamed through bullhorns and carried signs of condemnation at the demonstrations surrounding the house at 610 North Buchanan Boulevard. But why were they being thanked for not waiting? I wondered. What exactly were they "not waiting" for, the legal system to complete its investigation? The police probe was in full swing, the lacrosse team's season had been cancelled, and their coach was gone. Didn't the players deserve to have the wheels of justice turn fairly and deliberately in a way that would present the truth and expose the lies?

It was already apparent from the many comments that the Group of 88 had been publicly making that they were not even considering the possibility that the boys were innocent. Perhaps they weren't even interested in addressing that issue. After all, where would it have left them had they only been concerned with the innocence or guilt of the boys rather than the social issues that they seemed to be looking for an excuse to bring to the forefront? This was their chance to justify and publicize their interests, and the following words, also printed in the April ad, made that obvious: "The students know that the disaster didn't begin on March 13th and won't end with what the police say or the court decides. Like all disasters, this one has a history."

The "history" they were referring to was of racism and sexism and it was being attributed to this group of athletes simply because they were there, they had been accused, they were considered to be privileged, they were males, and more importantly, they were white. A group of well-educated "white jocks" was the perfect target for these "socially conscious" people to latch on to in order to prove what they had been trying to instill in the young minds of their students all along, that racism and sexism are still alive and thriving and that it was time to take action to stop it. How empowering that must have been for them. In all of their statements, those that made the papers and television news segments, others that were heard in classrooms and hallways and read in e-mails and on blogs, they assumed guilt. They seemed to want us to believe that they had taken the "politically correct" road by believing the alleged victim without question. Their minimal suggestions of "if this happened" and "if the boys are found guilty" were so overridden with essays about how racism and sexism are intertwined when white boys and black girls collide that their references to the possibility of innocence were barely noticed. You cannot suggest that people are innocent and then compose paragraph after paragraph describing why they are probably guilty. You just can't!

But, in spite of all of their backpedaling much later on, the most telling comment of all in their April ad, the one that prevents the Group of 88 from coming forward today to claim that they were not accusing the boys of the crime, was the following statement: "These students are shouting and whispering about what happened to this young woman and to themselves." That is a statement, not a mere suggestion, but a clear message that something *had*, in fact, happened to Mangum, and these professors, whose job it is to educate young minds, were actually thanking the university community, those who shouted through bullhorns and carried hate banners, for acting immediately and not waiting to see the evidence. They were thanking them for being irate and impatient about an investigation into an alleged crime. To me, their ad and their articles and public statements have all of the earmarks of a verbal lynching. Reading through all of their hyperbole about the wrongs of the Duke athletes and also the world as a whole, I began to feel as though I was drowning in a murky pool of agenda-filled mud. It was just unbelievable how far some of them went to gain support for their own causes at the expense of the lacrosse team.

Attorney Bill Thomas considered the Group of 88's statement, "Thank you for not waiting," "horrible." He said he interpreted it as "Thank you for not waiting to see what facts develop here. Thank you for jumping to conclusions based on race and social status." He added that "They should all be ashamed of themselves, every single one of them."

As vocal as the Group of 88 was, on the opposite end of the spectrum were university administrators who remained noticeably quiet, unable or unwilling to stand strong and defend the boys publicly. And because those individuals who were entrusted with our children sat back and said little to calm the flames that were festering, the Group of 88 was being perceived as the only voice being raised from within the halls of Duke. So outspoken were the members of this group that in a change of venue motion made by defense attorneys, their "We are listening" April ad was cited as evidence that pretrial publicity made it impossible for the boys to receive a fair trial in Durham.

While innocent onlookers began to swing with the pendulum of hate and vengeance, tensions were rising and more "rush to judgment" comments were made in favor of convicting the lacrosse team. One outspoken member of the Group of 88 was African American English Professor Houston A. Baker, Jr., who wrote a scathing letter on March 29, 2006, to the Duke administration just two weeks after the allegations were made, admonishing them for refusing to take "decisive and meaningful action." He wanted the boys punished, and his words surprised me, as I had hoped for more open-minded fairness from a professor at Duke. In his letter, he stated, "The lacrosse team . . . may well feel they can claim innocence and sport their disgraced jerseys on campus, safe under the cover of silent whiteness. But where is the black woman who their violence and raucous witness injured for life?" Baker went right to the heart of the issue with his "silent whiteness" comment. His focus on "whiteness" seemed an unlikely soapbox for someone whom I would presume has suffered racial discrimination at the hands of bigots during his lifetime. Yet there it was, appropriately in black and white, one against the other, a contrast of starkness, words of black on a background of white paper, a fitting symbol of the outrageous rhetoric that Baker was sending off to the Duke administration.

I was incredulous that a Duke professor would actually think those thoughts, much less put them in writing. But that was not even the worst of it. He continued on as though the lacrosse team was a band of racist athletes who had been inflicting slurs on black women all along:

"And when will the others assaulted by racist epithets while passing 610 Buchanan ever forget that dark moment brought on them by a group of drunken Duke boys? Young, white, violent, drunken men among us—implicitly boasted by our athletic directors and administrators—have injured lives." Baker even went as far as to suggest that the athletic department was duplicitous with their "deafening silence" since they had not come out publicly to crucify the lacrosse players.

It's true, the athletic department was somewhat quiet at first, but it didn't take very long for one of its most prestigious and credible members to come forward and say what needed to be said, and what should have been said by all representatives of the school. In a June 30, 2006, article on www.Bloomberg.com entitled "Duke's Krzyzewski Says Party Scandal Could Have Hit Hoops Team," famed Duke University basketball coach Mike Krzyzewski, as mentioned earlier, affectionately known as "Coach K," was quoted as saying that "while the school's lacrosse team party that ended in rape charges was 'stupid,' the university should have been more supportive of students as the scandal erupted." Adding that "There are going to be parties," he explained that "at those parties two things are going to happen: They're going to drink and have sexual activity. . . .What can you do so you don't create a situation that produces extreme activity like rape [and] binge drinking? That's what we as adults have to figure out." I admire Coach K's candor in recognizing the adults' role in how kids behave and also his understanding that some situations are fairly common among college kids today, such as underage drinking and sexual activity. Nobody is condoning it, but it is a fact of life that must be acknowledged and dealt with accordingly.

Coach K also commented that "the university should have provided more support for the lacrosse players and the rest of the students. They're your responsibility, whether they're lacrosse players, basketball players or normal students," he said, adding that "I would not have allowed as much media on our campus." Coach K also explained that he "drew the most important lessons about leadership from his alma mater, the U.S. Military Academy, where he learned that to succeed 'you have to fail, you have to make mistakes.'" That insight is what makes him such an outstanding coach as well as a fair and wise teacher. He did exactly what Brodhead and his fellow administrators failed to do: He stood by the athletes when they needed support the most, and he had the courage to do it publicly in the face of the negative media storm that was being directed at the boys.

Like many loyal Duke supporters and others who followed the case, Bill Thomas applauded Coach K's attitude and the fact that he treated the boys as though they were the university's "kids." Bill also commented that Duke administrators should have taken advice from the coach instead of acting on their "insane policy" of suspending the boys without any evidence of guilt, as well as disregarding the presumption of innocence and the boys' constitutional right to due process.

So, no, the Duke athletic department did not come out of their "deafening silence" to join the likes of Houston Baker and his 87 cohorts. Instead, they stood by their charges, the boys they had come to know as responsible individuals who had worked hard to achieve the respect of others. Unlike Baker, they didn't prejudge the boys or condemn them as "racists" as he did before even knowing the facts of the case. There was not one doubt in Baker's words, not one shred of justice or even-handedness in his statements. He was hell-bent on sending those "white" boys to jail once and for all. It didn't even seem to occur to him that they might be innocent. In fact, I dare say that it seems more likely that he hoped they weren't.

Baker's letter wasn't an isolated bit of anger spewed forth in a moment of weakness after such a serious allegation had been made. On the contrary, Baker's soapbox was somewhat taller than many of those other 87 members, but clearly, it was also much more unsteady. His venom wasn't really about David Evans, Collin Finnerty, or Reade Seligmann. It appeared to be about a deep-seated hatred for white people, and the lacrosse issue allowed Baker to unleash it, and "unleash" he did.

Appropriately, Duke Provost Peter Lange responded to Baker, saying that he was "disappointed, saddened, and appalled" by the letter. He told Baker that his words were "a form of prejudice" and "an act of prejudgment." However, that didn't stop Baker from continuing on with his outrageous tirade. To further bolster the fact that Baker's agenda was not about seeking justice, not equal justice for all anyway, and that it wasn't a knee-jerk reaction to an alleged criminal act, one need only read the following exchange that took place after months had passed and the truth behind the rape allegations was being brought to the surface.

The mother of an unindicted Duke lacrosse player wrote to Baker shortly before January 2007 more or less asking him for help and wondering if perhaps he had changed his mind now that it had become clear that the players were railroaded. This was her e-mail:

> Over the past eight months, much of the evidence has revealed that the three falsely indicted young men have been the victims of rogue D.A. Nifong. They have been denied due process and are the victims of a possible conspiracy. Whatever you believed in March, I am sure you must be questioning the actions of D.A. Nifong. Therefore, I respectfully request that you join Pres. Brodhead in asking for a special prosecutor. In addition, I respectfully request you petition Pres. Brodhead to allow Collin and Reade to resume classes this spring.
>
> Our paths may have been different, but I am sure all of us seek the truth and justice. This can only be accomplished with an

impartial prosecutor. Collin and Reade, along with Dave, have had to put their lives on hold due to a false accusation. I trust that with the filing of ethics charges by the NC State Bar [to be discussed in a later chapter] and the Conference of District Attorneys calling for D.A. Nifong to recuse himself, we can all agree that justice can best be served with Nifong's removal.

Baker's e-mailed response speaks volumes about his inability to look past his own hatred for whites to see the injustice that Mangum and Nifong had perpetrated on the lacrosse team.

LIES! You are just a provacateur [sic] on a happy New Years Eve trying to get credit for a scummy bunch of white males! You know you are in search of sympaathy [sic] for young white guys who beat up a gay man [sic] in Georgetown, get drunk in Durham, and lived like "a bunch of farm animals" near campus. I really hope whoever sent this stupid farce of an e-mail rots in . . . umhappy [sic] new year to you . . . and forgive me if your [sic] really are, quite sadly, mother of a "farm animal."

This is from a man who gets paid to teach some of our most intelligent kids! Can you imagine what the public's reaction would be if a white person called a group of black athletes farm animals? Where is the outcry from those who purport to be so sensitive to racial issues? It is intellectually dishonest for anyone who deems himself to be a defender of racial equality to ignore such a racist statement from anyone—black or white. It's hard to believe that Baker is allowed to continue in an occupation that entitles him to teach and mold young minds. It's even harder to believe that he is an English professor, considering the unintelligible way his letter was written. However, getting past the trivial issues to the heart of the matter, it isn't difficult to recognize that, sadly,

Baker has his own agenda and nothing that comes out of the lacrosse case will ever change his opinion of those "white boys."

Thankfully, Baker is no longer at Duke, having moved on to take a position at Vanderbilt University, but some of the others in the Group of 88 are leaving or have left their mark, or falling mark, so to speak. While talking to Professor Coleman, he mentioned that the only student he had spoken to during his committee's investigation was a lacrosse player named Kyle Dowd. The reason he had interviewed Dowd, he said, was because the committee had agreed to interview Dowd's mother and he came along with her. Coleman explained that Dowd was in a class at Duke and he had been doing fairly well academically, but the professor flunked him because he was a lacrosse player. Coleman considered the professor's behavior to be "absolutely outrageous." In reality, the allegation was that the professor had flunked two students, both lacrosse players, and also criticized them in front of the class. Coleman continued,

> I think any professor who confronted and tried to embarrass and call out kids in front of a class should be disciplined. I think that's totally inappropriate and shouldn't be tolerated on a university's campus. That's just inexcusable . . . but there are allegations that other professors were confronting the students, not flunking them, but talking about the lacrosse players with lacrosse players in the class. That's just cowardice in my view . . . prejudging their guilt and turning them into pariahs is inappropriate.

While at Duke, I had heard about what happened to Dowd. Apparently, visiting Professor Kim Curtis was at Duke teaching a "Politics and Literature" course when she joined the Group of 88. Two of her students were lacrosse players who purportedly had passing grades throughout the semester. However, when the term ended, she handed both of them, and only them, grades of F on their final assignments, allegedly without any justification at all. After graduation and complaints from the students and their families, Duke raised the grades to Ds, which the students still claimed was lower than what they deserved. Subsequently, one of the students, Kyle Dowd, filed a lawsuit against Duke and Professor Curtis, which may be the first of many stemming from the lacrosse fallout. Curtis's behavior, if true, is appalling. To punish students based on their affiliation with a sports team is no different than the racist behavior the boys were being accused of exhibiting toward Mangum.

Other professors also took actions that were way out of line. Reeve Houston, a professor of history, was teaching as part of his course issues involving "working class America." Students told me that he commented that the facts of the lacrosse case show that a rape definitely took place, and that semen had been found at the scene, meaning that someone ejaculated. Therefore, he allegedly said, a sexual assault had to have occurred. He apparently added that he was not there to condemn anyone, but he wanted to discuss it in the context of workers being exploited and the mistreatment of African American women by white men and their history of rape. There were four lacrosse players in his class, and they were so disturbed by Houston's comments that they walked out. Before one of them left, he said, "You'll see the truth." A female who played on the Duke University women's lacrosse team was in the class, and she broke out into tears due to the incident. This took place during the week of March 27, 2006, which ironically was "Sexual Awareness Week" on campus.

Another incident occurred on March 27, 2006, while three lacrosse players were on the quad on their way to class. They were walking out of an Alpine Bagels venue on campus and some African American kids kept shooting questions at them such as, "Why are you lying?" The team members kept walking, and the harassers gathered up approximately fifteen of their friends who began shouting at the players, "Why aren't you f—ing liars saying anything?" Then the mob started clapping, and they tried to push at the boys some fliers that had been circulating around campus regarding the night of March 13. The boys kept walking.

Another Group of 88 member, Associate Professor of African-American Studies, Mark Anthony Neal, commented to ESPN on April 3, 2006, that "For me, this is not simply a case of sexual violence or just a case of racism. It's a case of racialized sexual violence, meaning if it had been a white woman in that room, it would not have gone down the same way." In an attempt to explain how the lacrosse allegations clearly demonstrate his point of view, he added, "It's difficult for many folks to understand how race and gender came together in this case. You just can't pull them apart." In essence, Neal was implying that if two white strippers had shown up at 610 North Buchanan Boulevard on March 13, 2006, nothing bad would have happened because the majority of team members are white. He may be right, but not for the reasons he apparently attempted to espouse. I'd go as far to say that if any other black strippers had shown up at 610 North Buchanan, nothing bad might have happened; the "bad" element here is Mangum herself and her false allegations. Those allegations may have involved racism, but I believe that it was Mangum's and Roberts's racist behavior that was really at issue rather than the lacrosse team's.

It is important to note that the one black lacrosse team member, Devon Sherwood, was present during the dancers' performance and that while he left shortly after the dance ended, he stood strongly behind his forty-six teammates. In a comment he made during an interview with ABC's *Good Morning America* on October 31, 2006, he said he has never seen them exhibit any racist behavior in all the time he has been part of the team. Sherwood said he considers his teammates to be his "brothers." After Mangum made her claims of rape, he was quoted as saying, "When I came to Duke, I had one brother and now I have forty-seven." Surely if the lacrosse team was filled with white racists, Sherwood, who commented that he has a bond with his fellow team members that will last a lifetime, would have noticed it. But instead of recognizing that Sherwood's allegiance to the team should be taken as a message that all is not what it seems in the case against the boys, some have chastised and berated him for siding with the white kids.

After what I have learned, I must insist that this situation is not as simple as figuring out if an innocent black woman was terrorized by a bunch of rich white guys. What is becoming quite evident from the facts of this case is that the boys were the ones who were terrorized, and not just by a black exotic dancer who made false allegations against them but by so many different factions that it is difficult to keep track of them all. As I've said earlier, this is obviously an issue of race. If the situation had involved all black kids, all white kids, or a white victim and a black perpetrator, I doubt whether we would be hearing the multitude of racial slurs that Evans, Finnerty, and Seligmann have received merely because they are white. In fact, I know that to be the case, and I will expand on that later in chapter 9.

Another member of the Group of 88, History Professor William Chafe, penned a piece in Duke's newspaper, *The Chronicle*, on March 31, 2006, which included the following thoughts about the lacrosse party, "Whether or not a rape took place (and this is an issue that needs to be assessed objectively and with full fairness to everyone), there is no question that racial epithets were hurled at black people."

I am waiting for the objectivity to begin.

He continues, "Nor is there any question that white students hired a black woman from an escort service to perform an erotic dance."

Actually, there is a question. Dan Flannery was not aware that he had hired two black women. I'm still waiting for the objectivity to begin.

More from Chafe: "The intersection of racial antagonism and sexual exploitation is all too familiar." Perhaps it is worth remembering what Roberts said to the lacrosse players before the comment about the "white cotton shirt" was allegedly blurted out. She called the lacrosse players "limp-dick white boys." Is that not considered racial antagonism?

If you have followed the lacrosse story, you may have already heard about Professor Chafe, who as a member of the Group of 88, compared the alleged actions of the lacrosse team to the brutal murder of Emmett Till, a black teenager from Chicago who was beaten and shot in Mississippi for allegedly whistling at a white woman. Chafe used the reference to Till's story to help "put into context what occurred in Durham. . . ." He claimed that "The mixture of race and sex that transpired on Buchanan Boulevard is not new" and cited the "real issue" as being "how we will respond to this latest example of the poisonous linkage of race and sex as instruments of power and control." Chafe's attempt to use Emmett Till's story to put into context what happened at 610 North Buchanan Boulevard is akin to pouring gasoline on an already smoldering fire. There is no point to it, other than watching the flames take flight. So much for fairness and objectivity!

One of the most disturbing articles that I came across, besides those written by Chafe and Baker, was written by Karla Holloway, Professor of English at Duke and, ironically, at the time, the chair of the Campus Cultural Initiative Committee's subgroup on race. The essay, entitled "The Cultural Value of Sport: Title IX and Beyond" and dated Summer 2006, was located in Issue 4.3 of The Scholar and Feminist Online (S&F Online is available at www. barnard.columbia.edu), a site belonging to the Barnard Center for Research on

Women. In discussing her stance on the lacrosse team allegations, I find it necessary to include Holloway's entire first paragraph here, as it is an introduction that clearly defines her intent.

> When things go wrong, when sports teams beget bawdy behavior and debasement of other human beings, the bodies left on the line often have little in common with those enclosed in the protective veneer of the world of college athletics. At Duke University this past spring, the bodies left to the trauma of a campus brought to its knees by members of Duke University's Lacrosse team were African Americans and women. I use the kneeling metaphor with deliberate intent. It was precisely this demeanor toward women and girls that mattered here. The Lacrosse team's notion of who was in service of whom and the presumption of privilege that their elite sports' performance had earned seemed their entitlement as well to behaving badly and without concern for consequence.

The deliberateness of her words in stereotyping the members of the lacrosse team, as so many others had before her, leaves no doubt that she holds a strong sense of prejudice against college athletes as a whole, especially white male college athletes. Her words are nothing more than the thoughts of a close-minded pedagogue who views the alleged lacrosse incident as having been allegedly inflicted by an entire team, rather than by individuals. Apparently, Holloway has decided that they act and think in unison. If one is a racist, all are racists. If one rapes, all have raped. Her unbridled disdain for them made me wonder what might have happened in her own life to make her so bitter. I did some research and came across a site that held several reviews of one of her books, *Passed On*. (For more information, go to www.nathanielturner.com.) One critic, Jennifer K. Ruark, of

The Chronicle of Higher Education, made me understand where Holloway may have given birth to her hatred.

Apparently, Holloway had a son whom she and her husband adopted when he was four years old. As a teenager, Ruark explains, the boy began to exhibit signs of mental illness. After facing capital murder charges, he was convicted of rape and murder and was serving a ninety-five-year sentence until, in 1999, he was shot in the back while trying to escape from prison. Similar to the three lacrosse suspects' ordeal, the death of Holloway's son caused a media circus.

I am a compassionate man, and I am truly sorry for what Holloway was forced to endure. But how does someone suffer such a terrible tragedy so fraught with pain and humiliation and then advocate for the same experience to happen to someone else? At the very least, where is her compassion for the mothers of the boys on the lacrosse team? Of course, this doesn't even take into consideration the fact that the boys have been falsely accused of despicable crimes.

Holloway's thoughts on the legal system and its inability to handle the lacrosse situation thoroughly and appropriately come through clearly in her statement that "Judgments about the issues of race and gender that the lacrosse team's sleazy conduct exposed cannot be left to the courtroom." This leads me to doubt her own competence in having carried out her duties as chair of the race committee. The article does note, however, that she had been considering resigning from the "committee charged with managing the post culture of the Lacrosse team's assault to the character of the university." She states, "My decision has vacillated between the guilt over my worry that if not me, which other body like mine will be pulled into this service? Who do I render vulnerable if I lose my courage to stay this course? On the other side is my increasingly desperate need to run for cover, to vacate the battlefield, and to seek personal shelter." Holloway has actually taken on the role of a victim fraught with the unimaginable task of fulfilling a responsibility that, in truth, is no more daunting than what any other professor at Duke is expected to do as part of their tenure there. Is it possible that the lacrosse allegations were somehow forcing Holloway to relive her own past and the tragic events surrounding her son's conviction and subsequent death? In the same article, her explanation of the events that allegedly occurred on the night of March 13, 2006, reads as follows: "White innocence means black guilt. Men's innocence means women's guilt. These capacious categories, which were in absolute play the night of the team's drunken debacle, continue their hold on the campus and the Durham community."

I find that a bit too eerily simplistic, even devoid of rational analysis. Rather than acknowledging that the boys might be innocent, Holloway exploits this situation—ignoring any particulars (actual facts might get in the way of her academic posturing)—to further her own theories about how the issues involving race tend to polarize people. Her broad generalizations assume the lacrosse players' guilt, and she uses them as a springboard for airing her own grievances about campus politics. The sad part is that she will apparently always view black in conjunction with white, no matter the circumstances, as having some sort of racial overtones. Maybe that's because she views black and white cultures in a historical sense, i.e. white man's repression of black women.

If that were the case, had Mangum been white, Holloway's cause would have lost its meaning, because for her, the issue *is* only about race, not an alleged rape. If it had been anything more than that, she would not have berated the Duke women's lacrosse team when they, in a display of support for their brethren teammates at Duke, wore Evans's, Finnerty's, and Seligmann's jersey numbers on their sweatbands during a game. It is interesting to note that at the end of her essay, Holloway expressed her thanks to those who assisted her in drafting her essay, including William Chafe, the professor whose article so glibly compared the lacrosse players to Emmett Till's murderers. These extreme responses of Holloway and Chafe share the very unscholarly tendencies to sensationalize, over-generalize, and jump to some very hasty, inaccurate conclusions. I have been told that Holloway was the former Dean of Humanities and Social Studies under Chafe. Great minds think alike!

African American groups and any other person or entity that is against racial discrimination have truly missed a golden opportunity to use the Duke lacrosse case to further their cause. As attorney Bob Ekstrand put it, the Group of 88 "should be powerfully invested in this case because this is what happens to African Americans every day. While there is an impulse to sit back and let it happen to [white] boys for a change, they should be calling for the kind of justice that they would want for themselves." I have to agree. But, then again, it's easy for me to see things clearly since my only agenda is in seeking out the truth, as is Bob's. I am not here to find the boys innocent or Mangum guilty. As I mentioned in my opening paragraphs, I am only here to seek the truth, whatever that may be.

As is quite obvious to me by now, and as Professor Steve Baldwin suggested during one of our meetings, the Group of 88 is comprised of people who have a "very, very serious racial agenda." He explained that most of the time when they speak their minds and people get tired of hearing them, they move on. But then something like the lacrosse situation comes along, and, as Baldwin said, "they piggyback onto it." He called them "opportunists" and commented that he doubted that they "gave a damn about the lacrosse situation at all." He considered it an "opportunity for them to get their agenda out and talk about it." And while he made no bones about the fact that a "young woman with kids should not have to be in a situation where she has to go out and do that with her body to support her family," he was adamant in his position that the lacrosse incident "isn't a racial issue. The fact that [Mangum is] black is immaterial," he said. He makes an excellent point—the focus should be on whether or not a rape occurred, not the race of the people involved.

One thing that troubles me about the Group of 88 and the people who share their viewpoints is the position they all took. I find it hypocritical for them to say, "I'm concerned about race. I'm concerned about prejudice," and then tar these kids with the same brush before the investigation is even completed, primarily because they are white males. It seems to me that, in the big picture, from the university's standpoint, the group that made the most noise is the one that got heard. There are somewhere between six hundred and nine hundred faculty members in the arts and sciences, depending upon whether you count visiting professors. Thus, the Group of 88 is only a small part of the faculty. But, because they were the ones who spoke out the loudest, they were the ones who were heard. They were the ones who I believe really drove all the decisions that the university made. In other words, Duke allowed the tail to wag the dog.

Professor Baldwin shared with me his sentiments about Duke's handling of this situation. He said that although he has "strong opinions about Nifong . . . the bottom line . . . is that the university abandoned these kids. That to me is just unconscionable." He continued,

> You don't have to say they're innocent, you don't have to say we're going to do anything we can to get them off so they don't have to be punished. All you have to say is that they are our kids and we are going to make sure they have every opportunity to prove their innocence. You can say this anyway you want, you don't materially change anything, but you appear to be supporting the kids. I think everything would be a lot better if that had happened.

Professor Coleman also expressed his feelings about Duke along with his disappointment with the way things had been handled. "I love Duke. I think this is a great university . . . I think this whole thing has been unfortunate. I think that especially it's been unfortunate that these students got caught up in this and that more people, and this isn't just the university, didn't express concern about what was happening."

He added some final thoughts:

> I hope that some good comes out of this both in terms of what happened to the criminal justice system and in terms of the Duke community, that we look at what we did and decide that we need to protect each other better and have faith in each other. Maybe a little bit more faith than what we're showing in [the students involved in] this case. That when we've got forty-six students saying they didn't do anything and not a single one of them is saying anything happened, which is a pretty good indication that they may be telling the truth, we find a way to support them without saying we're indifferent to the truth; Because if a crime occurred, then we want that to be dealt with. But we don't want our students to get railroaded. And the problem with this case is that it's possible that an innocent student could have been railroaded and could have been convicted and sentenced to prison for life on this kind of [sham] evidence, and we've got to be concerned about that. That's why we have to care. And I think the University has to; that's one of its roles in the world, is to say those truths.

Fortunately, there are some representatives of Duke University who have maintained the voice of reason while demonstrating a strong sense of intellectual integrity and rational analysis during those difficult times. These include Jim Coleman, Steve Baldwin, Coach K, Paul Haagan, and others. It is highly unfortunate that the school administrators apparently chose not to follow their lead.

6

THE CONSPIRACY UNRAVELS

On June 19, 2006, counsel for Evans, Finnerty, and Seligmann again "requested various materials from Nifong, including a report or written statement" of Nifong's meeting with Dr. Meehan to "discuss the DNA results."

Another hearing was held on June 22, 2006, at which time Nifong told the court and the defense attorneys that the DSI report he had already turned over to the defendants contained all of the information that had been discussed at his meeting with Meehan. Nifong was ordered to turn over to the defendants several items, including DNA test results, witness statements, and reports of the results of any examinations or tests. However, due to Nifong's representation that the reports already contained everything that was said between Nifong and Dr. Meehan, the court did not specifically request memorializations of their discussions, because it would have been "redundant with the DSI report already given to defendants." That is what the court assumed based upon Nifong's claims.

After still not receiving what they had been asking for, on August 31, 2006, the Duke defendants filed a joint motion to force Nifong to turn over the entire DSI file and all underlying data in regard to the DNA testing in the lacrosse case, plus a memorialization of any relevant comments made by Dr. Meehan during his meetings with Nifong on April 10, April 21, and May 12, 2006.

Continuing with their quest to receive the information they had been requesting from Nifong, at a hearing on September 22, 2006, defense attorneys again requested "the results of any tests finding any additional DNA on [Mangum] even if it did not match any of the Duke defendants or other individuals for whom the State had provided DNA specimens" pursuant to Nifong's requests. In response to a question by the court, Nifong once again "represented that DSI's report encompassed all tests performed by DSI and everything discussed at his meetings with Dr. Meehan in April and May of 2006." Nifong was then ordered by the court to turn over DSI's complete file and all underlying data to the defendants.

On October 27, 2006, at another court hearing, Nifong turned over "1,844 pages of underlying documents and materials to the Duke defendants" pursuant to the court's September 22, 2006 order, but he did not provide a complete report from DSI setting forth the results of all of its tests and examinations, including the potentially exculpatory DNA test results, nor did he provide memorializations of what Dr. Meehan had said to him regarding the potentially exculpatory DNA results.

Also at that hearing, defense attorneys requested all statements that Mangum had made pertaining to the case. It was then that Nifong made a shocking announcement: he admitted that he had never interviewed Mangum about the events of March 13, 2006. David Evans's defense attorney, Joseph Cheshire, was appalled that Nifong had continued to proceed with the case against the boys when he had no idea what Mangum's version of the story really was. Under the circumstances, this is incredible to me. How could Nifong have said such damning statements about the boys, brought an indictment, and arrested them without so much as having a conversation with the alleged victim?

I have spoken to several prosecutors, and there is a consensus of opinion that prior to an indictment, the most prudent step to take is to talk to the victim to see if his or her statement deviates from their original complaint, and to evaluate the accuser's credibility as a witness. The fact that Nifong never felt it necessary to meet with the woman that he had been so vehemently defending is so stunning to me that I find it difficult to describe my reaction in words. It appears that either Nifong was hell-bent on pursing his premeditated course of action regardless of what Mangum said, or he avoided an interview with Mangum because he did not want to risk allowing any of the actual facts to get in his way.

Seven months into the case, this was the situation: Nifong had filled the airwaves with inflammatory and prejudicial information about the boys; he had refused to discuss any of their well-documented alibis with any of the defense attorneys; he had never interviewed Mangum to see if she could explain away the numerous discrepancies in her statements or other evidence in the case; he had instructed Meehan to only put positive results involving Mangum and the lacrosse players in the DNA report, which amounted to leaving out the exculpatory information that there was DNA in Mangum from numerous males who were not on the lacrosse team; and he directed Gottlieb to perform the photo identification session in a manner that violated every procedure set forth in North Carolina's laws and policies specifying how they should be performed to prevent any mistakes in the identification of a suspect. It was now abundantly apparent that Nifong's agenda had absolutely nothing to do with seeking justice.

On October 30, 2006, three days after the shocking revelation that Nifong had never met with Mangum, Kim Roberts appeared on ABC's *Good Morning America* and pulled another brick out of the already shaky foundation of Nifong's case. She began by describing the events that occurred after she left the party at 610 North Buchanan Boulevard on March 14, 2006. She said Mangum was "talking crazy," so Roberts attempted to get her out of her car by pushing on her leg and on her arm. Then came the shocker: Roberts said that she distinctly heard, as "clear as a bell, it's the only thing I heard clear as a bell out of her" as she put it, "Go ahead. Put marks on me. That's what I want. Go ahead." At the time that Mangum made these statements, Roberts had no idea that Mangum would later claim that she had been raped, and Roberts said that Mangum's odd behavior "chilled her to the bone," so she called the authorities. While Roberts's story appeared to be a revelation in the case, it is tempered by the fact that she does not make the most credible witness. Among other things, I thought she had earlier stated that she called the authorities because the boys were yelling racial slurs at her, or at Mangum, depending upon which one of her versions you prefer to believe. Now it was because of the way Mangum had been behaving. These discrepancies in her statements do not, in my opinion, extend Roberts much more credibility than Mangum. In addition, Roberts has had prior experience with the criminal justice system, which leaves some serious doubts about her credibility as a witness.

Kim Roberts, a.k.a. Kim Pittman, was convicted on December 11, 2001 for embezzling nearly $25,000, from Qualex, Inc., a Durham photo-finishing company where she worked as a payroll specialist. She received probation. She also has a more recent arrest under her belt. Eight days after the March 13, 2006, party, and shortly after giving her statement to the police about the events of that night, Roberts was picked up on a probation violation in relation to her 2001 conviction for failing to pay restitution to her former employer as required by the conditions of her probation, traveling out of North Carolina without permission from her probation officer, and neglecting to keep appointments with her probation officer. During her court appearance in Durham, Roberts turned to the cameras, made an obscene gesture, and stuck out her tongue. More interesting is this: On March 20, 2006, six days after the March 13 party, Roberts had called

Mangum's rape allegations a "crock," but on April 21, 2006, one month after Roberts's March 2006 arrest, during an interview with the Associated Press, she said, "In all honesty, I think [the boys are] guilty. And I can't say which ones are guilty . . . but somebody did something besides underage drinking. That's my honest-to-God impression." Defense attorneys have commented that "[Roberts] changed her story to gain favorable treatment in the criminal case against her." It certainly appears that way.

Here is some additional information to indicate that Roberts may have her own agenda besides seeing that the "truth" comes out now that she is caught up in the Mangum mess: A few weeks after the March 13, 2006, party, Roberts sent the following e-mail to a New York firm called 5W Public Relations that specializes in "crisis communication":

> I've found myself in the center of one of the biggest stories in the country. I'm worried about letting this opportunity pass me by without making the best of it and was wondering if you had any advice as to how to spin this to my advantage.

Ronn Torossian, 5W's president, said he replied, but got no response.

On December 14, 2006, all three defense teams jointly filed a "Motion to Suppress the Alleged 'Identification'" of David Evans, Collin Finnerty, and Reade Seligmann, purporting that the "'identification' process used by the State of North Carolina . . . violated due process, was inherently suggestive, was inherently misleading, and resulted in out-of-court identifications by the accuser that have been tainted and are unreliable." In simple terms, the defense attorneys were claiming that the procedure that was used in assisting Mangum in identifying the three lacrosse players from the mug shots as her attackers was unconstitutional, and, therefore, since the indictments against Evans, Finnerty, and Seligmann were based on the last of the series of three photo identification sessions that were all tainted, they should be suppressed, i.e. not allowed into evidence.

Let's step back in time for a moment and look at the facts upon which the motion was based. During the early morning hours of March 14, 2006, after Mangum was taken to the Duke University Medical Center emergency room, she met Durham Police Officer G.D. Sutton. She told him, in part, that she and "three other girls, Nikki, Angel, and Tammy" had performed at a bachelor party for "20 guys," that she was "sore and bleeding from her vagina," and that Nikki tried to convince her to have sex with one of the guys, but she refused.

Officer Christopher Day, a member of the Duke University Police Department who was present at the hospital, filed report #2006–01259 stating that on the above date, "a female was brought into the Emergency Department by Durham police in reference to a possible rape." The report continues as follows: "The female was picked up at the Kroger on Hillsborough Rd., and she was claiming that she was raped by at least 20 white males at 610 N. Buchanan Street."

After explaining that the police went to the alleged scene of the crime to investigate, the report continues: "The victim changed her story several times, and eventually Durham police stated that charges would not exceed misdemeanor simple assault against the occupants of 610 N. Buchanan. There were no charges filed by Duke Police Officers. No suspects have been identified at this time."

That was the first report in the case, and it states two important items: Mangum claimed to have been raped by "at least 20 white males," and "The victim changed her story several times." Right there, red flags were raised. Officer Day questioned the integrity of Mangum's statement. Why didn't anyone else? Getting back to Himan's affidavit in support of the NTO that ordered the lacrosse team to have mug shots taken and submit to DNA testing, and the critical information that he omitted from his statement, there is little doubt that the course of events in the investigation would have been steered in a completely different direction had all of the facts been included. The following is some of the evidence as also listed in the defense motion, which was missing from Himan's affidavit:

In Mangum's original statement on March 14, 2006, to Officer Sutton, she claimed that there were five men in the bathroom with her and that someone named Brett "penetrated her with his hands and penis." However, when Mangum told her story at the SANE facility on that same night, she said that "Brett and Nikki carried her back into the house," Adam kept her from leaving and Matt, after claiming that he was getting married, "raped her vaginally." Then she alleged that "Adam sodomized her," adding that "Matt [also] raped her orally." This time there was no mention of Brett sexually assaulting her.

Investigator Himan's report dated only two days later on March 16, 2006, stated that Mangum said that Adam (not Brett and Nikki) took her out of the car and brought her back into the house where "Brett [not Matt] first raped and sodomized her, followed by Matt [not Adam], and that Adam [not Matt] forced her to have oral sex." She also claimed that "Adam dragged her back to the car and wiped her off."

Sgt. J.C. Shelton arrived at the emergency room to meet with Mangum, and she told him that she was hired with one other girl, Nikki, to dance at the party. She said they "put on a show" and went to Nikki's car and that one guy came out to the car to ask if they would come back in, but she didn't want to. She claimed that she and Nikki argued after that and that she was dragged out of the car and groped by some of the guys from the party. She also told him that "no one forced her to have sex." Sgt. Shelton reported to his watch commander that Mangum recanted the rape claim, but within a few minutes, Mangum told the SANE doctor that she had, in fact, been raped. Sgt.

Shelton conveyed that to his watch commander and went back to talk to Mangum to ask her directly whether or not she had been raped. She told him she didn't want to talk anymore.

Additionally, the defense motion describes Mangum's own handwritten statement dated April 6, 2006, where she alleges that "Dan and Adam came to the car to apologize and bring her back inside," and that it was "Adam [not Matt] who was the attacker who said he was getting married," and that "Matt first raped and sodomized her, followed by Brett," another twisted version. She added that "Dan participated in beating her, and then Nikki and Adam took her back to the car." Those are just four different statements with four different versions of events, all from Mangum. But it doesn't end there.

The motion details a report from the physician at Duke University Medical Center's emergency room stating that on March 14, 2006, Mangum "specifically denied that she was hit by fists or hands" and that there was no evidence that she was injured about her neck, back, arms, or legs. However, on the following day, March 15, 2006, Mangum went to the University of North Carolina Medical Center where she claimed that "she had been knocked to the floor and that she hit her head on the sink, making her neck sore." Her only complaint that day was of "neck pain."

One more day passed, and according to the motion, on March 16, 2006, Mangum stated to Investigator Himan and Sgt. Gottlieb that she was "choked or strangled," but neither of their reports indicated that she had been "beaten or kicked" or that she fell and hit her head on the sink.

In short, as summarized in the defense motion, during the first thirty-six hours after Mangum alleged that she was raped she recanted her rape allegation, she claimed that she had been raped by twenty men, then five men, then two men, then three men; she claimed that she was carried from the car by Nikki and Brett, that

Nikki and Adam took her back to the car; and she claimed that she was dancing with three other women, and then claimed it was one other woman. She said she had been beaten, hit, and kicked, and choked and strangled, but then she denied ever being hit with fists or hands. She claimed that it was Matt who was getting married and then she said it was Adam. She told the forensic nurse that Matt raped her vaginally and orally, that Adam raped her anally, but didn't mention anything about Brett raping her. Yet she told others there that Brett raped her vaginally and at the same time didn't mention either Matt or Adam.

But here's a very interesting observation. Think back to chapter 1 to the first time that the claim of rape was made. Mangum was in Durham Access, and she was intoxicated, pretty messed up. The nurse didn't think Mangum was lucid, and she was trying to pull information out of her. Mangum didn't have much to say. So, the nurse decided to ask her if she was raped. It was the first time the word *rape* had entered the picture. It wasn't there during Roberts's 911 call. It wasn't there in the parking lot at Kroger. And it wasn't there on the way to Durham Access. It wasn't even there when she first arrived at Durham Access. It came out as an answer to the question, "Were you raped?" Mangum simply responded, "Yes." My cowriter, Stephanie Good, discussed with Bob Ekstrand her belief that the idea of rape was a thought planted into Mangum's apparently distorted sense of reality and that she latched on to it and told her story from there because she realized that it was her ticket out of the drunk tank. And, as with all tall tales, she couldn't keep her facts straight. In my many years as a trial lawyer, I have learned that if a person is telling the truth, the story will be consistent because there is only one story to remember. But if a person is lying and tells various versions of the same story to different people, it becomes very difficult for that person to keep the stories straight or remember them all.

Bob was actually excited when Stephanie first gave him her impression of what had transpired between the nurse and Mangum at Durham Access. His response when she mentioned it was, "Thank God! Thank God you get it!" He wasn't going to put the idea out there to her. He wanted to see if she had noticed it during our research, and she had. It was all too obvious. Incidentally, the thought had occurred to me as well.

Mangum is a very disturbed woman. I say this not out of mere opinion but from all of the facts that have come to light about her. I think it's time to give some background on Mangum before any further discussion about the defense motion.

Mangum comes from a working-class family in Durham. She had trained as a radio operator and navigator in the United States Navy, enlisting in 1996 and commencing her duty in 1997. Even though she had enlisted for two years of active duty and six years in the reserves, she was discharged from the service in 1998. I could not find the reason for her discharge, but what may have happened seems pretty clear. In 1997, Mangum married Kenneth Nathaniel McNeil. While still in the navy and married to McNeil, she allegedly began a relationship with another sailor with whom she had a child. The marriage ended, and six months later she was discharged from the service. Apparently, Mangum's discharge occurred less than nine months before the sailor's child was born. Mangum allegedly had another child with the sailor before their relationship finally ended. But there is more relevant information to follow.

Mangum has a pretty significant prior criminal history. In 2002, she was giving a lap dance to a taxi driver and "feeling him up" when she snatched his keys and stole his cab. After a high-speed chase that, according to the police report, lasted quite some time, she stopped the car. The pursuing officer assumed that she was not going to continue fleeing, so he approached her vehicle and "t[old] her to turn the car off and get out." She was actually sitting in the cab laughing as she "put the vehicle in reverse and backed across the road and into the woods." The officer, thinking Mangum was stuck, ran around his own vehicle to approach her when she put the cab into drive and headed straight for him. He was able to jump out of the way, but she smashed into the back of his patrol car. Mangum took off, and another police car entered the chase until Mangum was "boxed in." After she was apprehended, she was given an Alco-Sensor Test that gave a reading of .19. She passed out and was transported to the Duke University Hospital emergency room where she was arrested. Mangum was charged with felonious assault with a deadly weapon on a police officer; felonious larceny and felonious possession of a stolen vehicle; felonious speeding to elude arrest; driving while impaired and driving while her license was revoked; driving left of center; failure to heed a blue light and siren and reckless driving in wanton disregard to the rights or safety of others; driving the wrong way on a dual lane highway and open container after consuming alcohol; two counts of injury to personal property; and resisting a public officer. Amazingly, she was ultimately allowed to plead guilty to two misdemeanor violations (larceny and speeding to elude arrest), and also to driving while impaired and assault on a government official. She was sentenced to serve jail time, but the multiple sentences were suspended, except for serving three weekends, amounting to a mere six days. She was also given twenty-four months supervised probation. On May 11, 2005, her probation ended. Her sentence was incredibly lenient for those charges, especially considering the underlying facts.

The most interesting bit of information about Mangum's past can be found in Reade Seligmann's "Motion to Suppress Identification Testimony" filed on May 1, 2006. According to the police report attached to the motion, on August 18, 1996, Mangum made an accusation that was all too similar to the one in the current case, claiming that three years earlier when she was fourteen years old, she was raped and beaten by three men whose names and addresses (with the exception of one address) she gave to police. She was asked to provide a "chronological order statement," but never did. Perhaps she thought the same thing would happen in this case, that she would be asked to return to pursue her case and she could just go home and forget about it. If that's true, she obviously didn't know she was dealing with one man who has a reputation as being a Duke-hating cop and another who is viewed as a rogue prosecutor with a personal agenda in which she would be central to his plan.

Reportedly, Mangum was engaged to her former husband, Kenneth McNeil, seventeen years her senior, when she confessed to him that the man involved in the earlier alleged rape was seven years her senior and was abusive, jealous, and controlling. She also claimed that he had passed her around to his friends, all black males, letting them take turns having sex with her. According to McNeil, he believed that she had been raped, and he encouraged her to file the police report, but she never pursued the claim.

According to an August 25, 2006, *New York Times* article entitled "Files From Duke Rape Case Give Details but No Answers," Mangum recently told Durham investigators that she dropped the earlier rape case after police told her it would be hard to prove and that she had also been told that "all the men were already imprisoned for other crimes."

Also noted in Seligmann's motion was another claim that Mangum had made in the past. "On June 16, 1998, [Mangum] state[d] under oath that her husband, Kenneth Nathaniel McNeil, took her into the wood[s] and threatened to kill her." However, "she failed to appear at a hearing" scheduled for June 23, 1998, "to prove her allegations. Thus, the matter was dismissed." McNeil denied Mangum's claims. The two had been married for seventeen months at the time that the allegations were made.

Another interesting piece of information came from Mangum's mother, who told *Essence Magazine* that Mangum had a nervous breakdown last year.

Judging from Mangum's past history, her behavior on the night of March 13, 2006, and the contradicting statements that she gave to the police, the people at Durham Access, and the SANE nurses and doctor, it is apparent that she has significant psychological problems. Of course, I can't assess Mangum's mental state, but one telling observation can be made. It is extremely difficult for defense attorneys to obtain the psychiatric records of an alleged rape victim. The judge generally reviews them *in camera*, meaning privately without the attorneys or jury present. If the judge deems the information relevant to the case, he turns it over to the attorneys. I have been informed that Mangum's psychiatric records have been turned over to the defense, and the implications of this are very powerful. The records, however, are under seal, which means the information cannot be released to the public.

What might it mean to this case that the records have been turned over? If Mangum has some type of disorder that causes delusions or other behavior to indicate that she has breaks with reality, it could be significant because, if that is the case, she can't be relied upon as a credible witness. And, if that's the case, what does this say about Nifong? What if Nifong knew Mangum has some type of disorder, but did not reveal that information as well? He must surely have been well aware of this fact, because if the defense attorneys have her psychiatric records, then he must also have received them. It is mind-boggling to think that Nifong had all of the DNA test results, and that he had to be aware of the substantial amount of other evidence that weighed strongly in favor of exonerating the boys, as well as knowing that his star witness, Mangum, might have a major problem in maintaining her credibility, and he still proceeded to put all of these things aside as though they didn't matter. Did he think that by pressing forward with the case even in the face of all of this that he might be able to pressure the boys into entering a guilty plea so that his questionable conduct would never be discovered?

Another variation of Mangum's story as noted in the December 14, 2006, defense's "Motion to Suppress the Alleged 'Identification,'" is that at the University of North Carolina Medical Center on March 28, 2006, she told doctors that "when she had been assaulted, 'she fell and slipped' and hit her knee." Less than one week later, on April 3, 2006, Mangum told doctors that her attacker had "squeezed her neck and then kicked her in the back of the neck."

However, as mentioned earlier and also noted in the defense motion, on April 6, 2006, Mangum, in her own handwritten statement, claimed that she was kicked in the "behind" and her back prior to being sexually assaulted. She also stated that after the assault, she was "hit in the face and kicked by Dan and Brett." There was no mention in that statement of either being choked or strangled even though she did state that to Investigator Himan and Sgt. Gottlieb on March 16.

The conflicting statements made by Mangum should have raised some serious red flags to any prosecutor who was interested in seeing that justice was served. On the remote chance that Nifong missed those flags that were not only waving in front of him but also draped over his head, the following information should have made bells and whistles, if not foghorns, go off.

Two sets of descriptions of Mangum's alleged assailants were available in the police reports, Investigator Himan's and Sgt. Gottlieb's. Himan's handwritten notes, taken from Mangum's statement, differed from his typewritten record that named Mangum's attackers as "Adam, Brett, and Matt." There were no descriptions contained in the typed report. However, in Himan's handwritten notes, Mangum described her alleged attackers in the following way: Adam was "a short white male with brown fluffy hair, red cheeks, and a chubby face." She described Matt as "'heavy set' with a 'short hair cut' and weighing 260 lbs. to 270 lbs." Brett was described as "chubby," and Mangum "claimed that she saw a picture of him."

Sgt. Gottlieb did not take any notes during his March 16, 2006 interview with Mangum and only prepared a report at a much later date. Interestingly, his report was not provided to Nifong until sometime after June 22, 2006, and then to the defendants on July 17, 2006, so there's no telling how much time had passed before he finally prepared it. Among other things, his report contained the following descriptions of the suspects that Mangum had allegedly given: "W/M, young, blond hair, baby faced, tall and lean"; "W/M, medium height (5'8"+ with Himan's build), dark hair, medium build, and had red (rose colored) cheeks"; "W/M, 6+ feet, large build, with dark hair." Gottlieb did not use names to identify which of the descriptions belonged to which of the "named" alleged suspects.

Analyzing the descriptions, it is clear that they differ significantly:

HIMAN:
"short white male with brown fluffy hair, red cheeks, and a chubby face"
"'heavy set' with a 'short hair cut' and weighing 260 lbs to 270 lbs."
"chubby"

GOTTLIEB:
"W/M, young, blond hair, baby faced, tall and lean"
"W/M, medium height (5'8"+ with Himan's build) dark hair, medium build, and had red (rose colored) cheeks"
"W/M, 6+ feet, large build, with dark hair"

Clearly, Himan's descriptions do not match those Gottlieb pulled out of his memory bank at a later date. It is difficult to imagine that the investigating officer in charge of supervising the case did not think it was important enough to take specific notes during the interview.

As the motion notes, the descriptions of the three indicted lacrosse players either do not correspond with the ones in Himan's and Gottlieb's notes, or they are too vague to pinpoint any one lacrosse team member. For example, "Reade Seligmann is a white male with dark hair who was 6'1" and weighed 215 pounds." His description closely matches twenty-eight other Duke lacrosse team members. "Collin Finnerty is a white male who was 6'5", weighed 215 lbs., has reddish hair, and has a prominently freckled face." "Dave Evans is a white male with brown hair who was 5'9" and weighed 185 lbs."

Based on the above information, including the multiple statements that Mangum had given and the differing descriptions of the alleged suspects, there was no valid basis to justify the granting of the NTO that covered forty-six males. It is clear that critical information was omitted so that the affidavit would support what the police or the District Attorney's office wanted the judge to believe and made it more likely that he would issue the NTO.

Bob Ekstrand pointed out that the prosecution would claim that they don't have to include exculpatory information in their affidavit for an NTO application for a warrant under the Constitution or state statutes, so they don't have to reveal that Mangum told several different stories. However, Bob said that his own view is quite different. He explained that "an NTO is obtained ex parte, meaning no opposing counsel is involved, which under ethics rules requires that you have an obligation to the tribunal to tell the whole story. You can't abuse the fact that you have an opportunity to get an ex parte order by telling the judge only information that is favorable to you while concealing details that are obviously important to the judge's consideration in his decision. However, some people feel that they can do just that."

On Friday, December 15, 2006, the day after the defense filed their

"Motion to Suppress the Alleged 'Identification,'" Dr. Brian Meehan, the head of DSI, the second laboratory to perform DNA testing at the request of Nifong, was called as a witness at a pre-trial hearing to testify about the circumstances surrounding the DNA testing. During his testimony, under brutal cross-examination by Brad Bannon, one of David Evans's attorneys, Meehan revealed the agreement that he and Nifong had made on April 21, 2006, not to report any DNA results that were favorable to the lacrosse players.

Bannon was seen as a true hero by all except the prosecution that day. He had undertaken the laborious task of reviewing the thousands of pages of DNA data until he knew it cold, and when he stood up and began questioning Meehan, it was without any advance notice that Meehan would even be testifying. Yet he managed to obtain a confession from the DNA expert that he and Nifong had, in essence, conspired to withhold exculpatory evidence from the defense.

The three accused players, Evans, Finnerty, and Seligmann, and their families were all present, together in court for the first time, when Meehan dropped this bombshell. As bad as many aspects of this case were, this was just surreal. To think that Nifong knew all along that there was exculpatory evidence and he had made a deliberate and calculated attempt to cover it up is just shocking beyond belief. Worst of all was the fact that he knew it before he indicted the three boys, and he still went ahead and pursued his case—based on these bogus allegations.

The irony here is that Nifong had been working all along under the cloak of a reputation for generally being a tough prosecutor with a reasonable sense of ethics. He built this reputation as a tough but honorable prosecutor during a period spanning more than a quarter of a century, and as far as I could find, he had never been called out on anything. He has stated that he has always given open-file discovery in all of his cases, even long before there was a statute requiring it. So the question becomes, now that there is actually a law requiring him to do what he claimed to be doing all along, what happened in this particular case? Did he deliberately choose to avoid his obligation to comply with it, or are we to believe that this is merely a one-time slip up, a mere oops? After all, the defense submitted a discovery request that has been on the table for almost a year and there is only one way to handle it properly.

As Bob Ekstrand and I discussed, if you have the information, you simply turn it over to opposing counsel. And, if you have it in your head and you haven't written it down, you write it down and turn it over to opposing counsel. That is what the rules of legal ethics require lawyers to do in order to comply with this statutory obligation.

It is inconceivable that Nifong would have gone to all that trouble to repeatedly withhold the DNA results, time after time, from the defense attorneys and the judge, without any calculated intent. He knew enough to tell Meehan to only include positive results in the report. He knew enough to be specific about what information he thought was relevant to include and what was to be left out. And, for some reason, Meehan deviated from his own policy, and in spite of allegedly never doing it before, went along with Nifong and left out this exculpatory evidence. It just seems implausible that it was one big oversight or merely a misunderstanding. It seems much too calculated a move to believe that this was the first time that Nifong had ever done anything like that, whether it was withholding exculpatory evidence or otherwise.

7

PROSECUTORIAL MISCONDUCT

As the evidence continued to expose the lies, the final ax was about to fall on Nifong's credibility and possibly on his case. On December 21, 2006, someone from the Durham District Attorney's office interviewed Crystal Gail Mangum—for the *very first time*. Linwood Wilson, a gospel singer/former police officer/retired private investigator, and Nifong's chief investigator in the Duke Lacrosse Case, met with the alleged victim to hear her version of the events that transpired on the night of March 13 and early morning hours of March 14, 2006. Wilson, after spending seven years in retirement, was hired by Nifong in 2005 to help track down people who had written bad checks. He was assigned to the lacrosse case as soon as Nifong took over supervision of it. During Wilson's meeting with Mangum, astoundingly, she allegedly changed her story yet again, altering numerous material details, including the timeline of events, the identity of her alleged attackers, as well as how she was allegedly assaulted. Significantly, this time she stated that she didn't know if anyone had penetrated her vagina with a penis. She also stated that Seligmann did not participate in any part of the alleged assault.

Her newest version of the story presented yet another piece of the puzzle that didn't fit with the actual and documented timeline of events, the pictures, Bissey's statement, or the accused players' alibis. In fact, Mangum's new claims were as follows: that the attack occurred between 11:35 p.m. and midnight; that it was not "Reade Seligmann who stood in front of her and made her commit a sex act," and that instead, it was David Evans; the revelation that "Seligmann did not commit any sex act on her"; the recanting of her statement that her attacker had a moustache; the recanting of her previous statements that "'Matt,' 'Adam,' and 'Brett' were three separate people," claiming now "that they were only two people"; the recanting of her statements that "each attacker used a separate name," now claiming "that Dave Evans used three (and possibly four) names, and that Collin Finnerty did not use any name during the attack." She also recanted her "numerous statements that she was certain that two of her attackers used their penises to penetrate both her vagina and her rectum . . . now claiming that she cannot be sure about penile penetration at all."

It was an entirely new version of events and, if none of the earlier contradicting evidence had made Nifong drop the charges, Mangum's latest story should definitely have pushed him to toss the whole case out. But he didn't toss it. In his own distorted way of thinking, merely made the case a little easier for him to win. On Friday, December 22, 2006, Nifong, having been left with no other choice, dropped the rape charges. Amazingly, sexual assault and kidnapping charges remained, even against Reade Seligmann, who had well-documented evidence that he was not even at the party when the crimes were alleged to have occurred.

To better appreciate how any charges remained and how Seligmann's charges were not dropped even though Mangum stated that he did not participate in the alleged attack, it is necessary to understand what the charges mean. The State of North Carolina still goes by the old definition of rape, which only includes penile penetration of the vagina. Under this application of the law, penile penetration of any other part of the body falls under the category of sexual offense. So, once Mangum claimed that she didn't know if anyone had vaginally penetrated her with his penis, Nifong had *no choice* but to drop the rape charges. However, basing his actions on all of Mangum's other claims, Nifong left the sexual assault and kidnapping charges in place. It seems obvious that Nifong would run into serious problems continuing with his case against Reade Seligmann in light of the fact that Mangum had eliminated him from participation in any of her sexual offense claims, but that is not necessarily the case. According to Bob Ekstrand, "It is a mistake to think that anyone who didn't touch Mangum is safe. If Nifong can prove that a sexual assault and kidnapping did occur, which is extremely doubtful, Seligmann could be convicted as an accomplice just for being in the room." Ekstrand also stated that Nifong doesn't even have to amend the indictment. He can simply transform it to indicate accomplice liability. However, Nifong would have a hard time overcoming Seligmann's rock-solid alibi.

Several reports have indicated that Linwood Wilson, Nifong's investigator who allegedly took Mangum's latest statement, has a somewhat checkered past of his own. In a January 24, 2007, article on www.newsobserver.com entitled "Ethics of Nifong's Detective at Issue," it was reported that Wilson, "the only full-time investigator on Nifong's staff, was investigated twenty years ago 'on suspicion of making false statements on the witness stand and setting up an illegal telephone tap, according to his file at the state agency that licenses private investigators.'" While there were never any criminal charges brought against Wilson in the incident, defense attorneys have also questioned his credibility. Due to his allegedly less than stellar past, defense attorneys have questioned whether his notes from the interview with Mangum were concocted in order to make her story fit more in line with Nifong's portrayal of the case. After all, it isn't a giant leap to go from conspiring with a DNA expert to withhold exculpatory evidence to fudging a statement taken by a creative investigator from a less than credible witness.

During Wilson's interview with Mangum, she changed her story so significantly that it would be very difficult for any prosecutor to rehabilitate her as a witness. It is highly unlikely that any juror would believe her story given the fact that she has told so many variations of it, much of which is totally inconsistent, especially when held up against the exculpatory evidence and well-documented alibis of the suspects.

For example, Reade Seligmann had several pieces of hard evidence that supported his alibi. He produced his cell phone records that reflected that he had been using his phone during the time that Mangum originally claimed the alleged assault was taking place. There were the time-stamped photos taken during and after the party. Seligmann produced a Wachovia ATM photo that proved he was nowhere near 610 North Buchanan when Mangum was allegedly being attacked. He had a sworn statement from taxi cabdriver, Moez Elmostafa, who confirmed that he picked up Seligmann and a friend that night, at what time he picked them up, and where he took them. There was also a record of Seligmann's own secure dorm card showing that he was already back at his dorm while the alleged events that Mangum claimed in her original statement would have still been occurring. This was only some of the evidence offered to Nifong early in the case by the defense attorneys, evidence that he refused to view or even acknowledge.

In regard to Seligmann's alibi, according to an April 26, 2006, *Time* article entitled "Why the Duke Cabdriver Could Also Help the Prosecution," Moez Elmostafa, told investigators that he picked Seligmann and a friend up at 610 North Buchanan at 12:19 a.m. on March 14, 2006, and dropped them off at a campus dorm at 12:40 a.m. after making several stops. One of the stops was at the ATM machine. Elmostafa "returned to the house at 12:50 a.m. to pick up four more players. . . ." Elmostafa also told *Time* that police investigators asked him if he had been paid to provide an alibi for Seligmann. Of course, he had not. He was simply telling the truth. In addition,

Seligmann's statement was clearly supported by the ATM photo as well as the record from his secure dorm card.

Curiously, there is yet another twist to this story regarding this cabdriver. In May of 2006, approximately two months after Mangum's allegations, Elmostafa was arrested on an old warrant stemming from a 2003 shoplifting charge. The warrant accused him of stealing five purses from a Durham department store. It was alleged that security cameras had filmed a woman taking the merchandise and entering Elmostafa's cab. Elmostafa stated that he had merely picked up the woman who happened to be the shoplifter at the store and driven her home. He later assisted the store security guard in locating the woman. She had, in fact, pleaded guilty, and Elmostafa was never contacted any further about the case, so he thought he was done with it. Seligmann's former attorney, Ernest Connor, considered Elmostafa's arrest to be nothing more than the intimidation of a witness. The timing is certainly curious under these circumstances.

According to a January 24, 2007, article on www.newsobserver.com entitled "Ethics of Nifong's Detective at Issue," Linwood Wilson "played a key role in the May arrest of [Elmostafa]." Apparently, after Elmostafa came forward to corroborate Seligmann's alibi, Wilson came up with the three-year-old unserved warrant related to the shoplifting charges. Elmostafa "maintained that he knew nothing about the theft, but the warrant remained outstanding." The May 2006 arrest occurred after Wilson informed Nifong about the warrant. In an August 2006 trial, Elmostafa was acquitted while "Wilson and other lacrosse investigators look[ed] on from the gallery."

Even if no taxi driver had come forward, Mangum's statements made during the photo identification session in which she identified Seligmann should have been more than enough to exonerate him. However, as with everything else, Nifong totally disregarded the following important facts. During the PowerPoint presentation on

April 4, 2006 in which she purported to identify Seligmann, Mangum stated that he was the one standing in front of her who made her "perform oral sex on him." She also identified Seligmann as "Adam." However, in Himan's notes, she reportedly described Adam as a "white male, short, red cheeks, fluffy hair, brown, chubby face." Seligmann is 6'1" and weighs 215 pounds. He's anything but short and chubby, and he has black hair, not brown. Furthermore, when Mangum identified Seligmann in the photos that she was shown on March 16, 2006, she was only "70%" sure she "recognized [him] as having been at the party"; but she couldn't remember where at the party she saw him. Additionally, Mangum, in one of her various statements, specifically described what Adam had done to her during the alleged attack, right down to him "dragging [her] out to the car because [her] legs wouldn't move." As mentioned earlier, according to the witnesses, the time-stamped photos, and Seligmann's own documented alibi evidence, it was impossible for him to have still been at 610 North Buchanan at the time Mangum claimed that the alleged attack had occurred. It was equally impossible that he would have been involved in her attack and still been making and receiving the phone calls that were documented on his cell phone records for that time period.

Collin Finnerty claims to also have a well-documented and iron-clad alibi. He was allegedly at a restaurant called the Cosmic Cantina when the alleged rape was said to have occurred. According to news reports, his parents have said that there are witnesses, receipts, cell phone records, and a dorm card that all prove his whereabouts and what time he was there, any of which would clearly prove his innocence. He has also easily passed a polygraph exam. Further, Finnerty did not match any description that Mangum gave throughout all of her statements, especially of the person she claimed had been her second assailant, "Brett." He was described as "chubby." When Mangum identified Finnerty during the PowerPoint presentation, she claimed he was the "second one" to penetrate her. At 6'5" and 215 pounds, Finnerty is anything but "chubby."

David Evans's picture had been shown to Mangum twice on March 21, 2006, and she did not recognize him. She was shown his picture again on April 4, 2006. This time, she viewed his photo during the PowerPoint presentation and that was when she suddenly decided that she recognized him as one of her attackers with "90%" certainty, except for one thing—his moustache. She claimed he had one on the night of the party. Photos taken on the days before and after the party clearly confirm that Evans did not have a moustache on the night of March 13, 2006. He also passed a polygraph exam with flying colors.

On December 28, 2006, the North Carolina State Bar filed a seventeen-page formal ethics complaint against Nifong citing as "misleading commentary" the inflammatory and misleading statements that Nifong had been making to the media about the Duke lacrosse team members. The complaint also accused Nifong of "dishonesty, fraud, deceit, or misrepresentation" in regard to the statements he made about the possibility that Mangum's alleged attackers used condoms, in spite of the SANE report that had stated otherwise.

The next day, December 29, 2006, the North Carolina Conference of District Attorneys publicly urged Nifong to remove himself from the case.

At the same time that it was becoming clear that Nifong's case against the lacrosse players was falling apart, others who had been running with the pack of wolves pushing for a conviction were starting to look for subtle ways to change their direction and correct their course of actions. On January 3, 2007, Duke University President Richard Brodhead, on the advice of Vice President for Student Affairs, Larry Moneta, announced that "the right and fair thing to do is to welcome back Reade Seligmann and Collin Finnerty to resume their studies at Duke for the spring semester."

At first glance, this may seem like a victory for the accused boys. However, it is too little and far too late. First, the boys should not have been suspended in the first place. Members of the Duke administration, and President Brodhead in particular, consistently attempted to justify the suspension of the boys by pointing out that it is school policy to suspend any student who is charged with a felony. However, a policy is just that—a policy, not an iron-clad rule. Generally, policies are viewed more as guidelines, with each case being considered separately based upon its specific factual circumstances.

The Duke administration knew in the early stages, well before it decided to suspend the two indicted students, that there was a substantial amount of evidence that strongly favored their innocence. The school's president and other leaders within the administration chose to ignore that evidence, and instead chose to rely on the false and incendiary statements made by Nifong. In short, they chose not be believe their own students, whose stories were corroborated by a significant amount of objective evidence, including pictures, documents, and testimony from numerous other witnesses.

At the very least, the administrators had more than sufficient evidence in front of them to delay any action against the students pending further review. Instead, they buckled under the wave of extreme political correctness, and they were more concerned about publicity and media perception than they were about the lives and the welfare of the students with whom they had been entrusted.

Second, even if we were to assume that the administrators' action to suspend the students in the spring was not unreasonable under the circumstances, they certainly should have invited them back to school during the summer when the evidence in the case against them was surfacing and unraveling in the media. That way, they would not have missed the fall semester, assuming they would have been inclined to return to Duke after what they had experienced there.

If the administrators contend that they could not have invited the students to resume their education until after the rape charges were formally dropped, their position is disingenuous. This position is totally inconsistent with their stated "policy" that they were supposedly following when they suspended the boys in the first place. When Brodhead finally did the right thing and invited the boys to reenroll at Duke after the rape charges had been dropped, the felony charges of sexual assault and kidnapping still remained. Thus, the boys were still theoretically in the same position they were in when the school suspended them, because they were still being charged with serious felonies.

What concerns me gravely is this: Brodhead apparently did not consider how "wrong and unfair" his decision was to send those boys home without affording them the presumption of innocence in the first place, especially when he had so much evidence in support of their innocence. This is just weak, a glaring demonstration of a total lack of leadership, if not human decency.

Not surprisingly, Seligmann and Finnerty did not return to Duke for the spring semester. As much as I love Duke, I can't really blame them. As a parent, I would not have sent my son back to that campus environment considering all of the horrors that those boys endured and the lack of support that the university afforded them prior to their suspensions.

As disappointing as Brodhead's actions were, it was shocking to me that there were faculty members who thought that Brodhead was being too kind and lenient toward the students. As a direct result of Brodhead's invitation to Seligmann and Finnerty to return to Duke, Karla Holloway was so upset that she finally resigned as chair of the race committee. Citing Brodhead's decision to invite the boys back to the university to continue with their educations, she submitted her letter of resignation, stating the following: "The decision by the university to readmit the students, especially just before a critical judicial decision on the case, is a clear use of corporate power, and a breach, I think, of ethical citizenship." She continued, "I could no longer work in good faith with this breach of common trust." Holloway also expressed her criticism of the administration for not being more supportive of her and her 87 cohorts: "The public support [the administration] has extended to these students has been absent in regard to faculty who have been under constant and often vicious attack." Holloway's last comment can be easily interpreted to mean that the vicious attacks unleashed on the boys by her "group" should have been publicly supported by Brodhead, and the fact that they were not, left the group open to verbal assaults. If that was her implication, that statement couldn't be further from the truth. The administration's lack of criticism of the actions of the Group of 88 led many people to believe that Brodhead and his colleagues actually supported their position, which implied guilt on behalf of the accused lacrosse players. But Holloway, in an apparent attempt to avoid having to answer for her statements and unwilling to engage in any rational discussion, much less respond to criticism once the truth began to surface, began playing the sympathy card. She resigned from the committee in a huff of righteous indignation and whined about a lack of support from the administration because the school finally did the right thing with respect to the real victims in the case.

Holloway was certainly no victim, and her strong words against the lacrosse team were not misinterpreted. It was clear that she had it in for the Duke athletes in general. Her words are intellectually dishonest. They are nothing more than the comments of an apparent race baiter who was upset because nobody bought into what she was attempting to sell. While she was in a resigning mood, why stop with the committee? Why not resign from the university all together?

On January 11, 2007, pursuant to the new information obtained from Linwood Wilson's interview with Mangum, defense attorneys filed a "Supplement to the Motion to Suppress the Alleged Identification," laying out additional reasons why the photo identification should be suppressed. The motion is still pending.

On January 12, 2007, Nifong asked the State Attorney General, Roy Cooper, to remove him from the Duke Lacrosse Case and appoint a special prosecutor to take it over. In the face of the serious charges brought against him by the North Carolina State Bar, Nifong apparently took this step after finally obtaining some rational advice from a reasonably competent lawyer.

8

THE INCONVENIENT TRUTH

Much to my chagrin, it has become all too apparent to me that hypocrisy has been allowed to reign in the halls of Duke, overshadowed and underscored by the arrogance of some seemingly highly educated faculty members and students. Those of us who have followed the lacrosse case objectively have come to realize that a terrible injustice has been served up on Dave Evans, Collin Finnerty, and Reade Seligmann. There is no doubt that they broke some rules. They hired strippers and served alcohol to underage fellow students. That was a matter that should have been appropriately addressed internally. However, the truth is that if Mangum hadn't made her alleged claims of rape, the lacrosse team's party would have gone unnoticed like many other college parties across the country—unnoticed by all except perhaps for Bissey, the guy who sat watching from his porch next door.

Violating school rules and breaking the law fall into two hugely different categories. It is a fact of life that kids sometimes break rules. That is part of their nature as human beings, and it is also a part of growing up. Hopefully, they don't cause permanent damage to themselves or others while doing so. Those of us who were lucky enough to get through our rites of passage without leaving a trail of hurt or criminal convictions in our wake consider those indiscretions to be part of life's lessons. It is through those lessons that we mature and learn to be better people. I can only wonder what the lives of Evans, Finnerty, and Seligmann would have been like right now had it not been for the tragic events that were bestowed upon them by an extremely troubled young woman. David would have probably been working hard at the job that was waiting for him after graduation, while Collin and Reade would most likely be keeping up with their studies and sharing victories on the lacrosse field with their Blue Devil teammates. Duke would not have been tarnished by this tragic atrocity, and the alcohol and stripper parties would have continued without much attention.

The boys will survive, but they have been scarred. My hope is that they will be able to overcome those scars that Mangum, Gottlieb, Nifong, Brodhead, the Group of 88, the potbangers, and many others have inflicted on them. This is one heck of a life lesson for those boys, and I am confident that they will use it to their advantage in the years to come. There is much to learn from this tragedy for each of them. I pray that they will be able to remain optimistic and non-judgmental, that they will not be filled with anger and hate, and most importantly, that they will be able to come to the point where they can trust again. In light of what has happened to them and the way they have been mistreated, it won't be easy. These young men had worked very hard to earn their tickets into a school like Duke, and just by doing that, it is clear what kind of individuals they are. The way they have handled this travesty of justice gives us some insight into how they are coping now.

In a January 15, 2007, interview with *Newsweek* entitled "In Scandal's Shadow," Reade Seligmann gave readers a glimpse of life after being charged with rape. He described waiting at a New Jersey law firm with his dad, Philip, to find out if Mangum had identified him as one of her alleged attackers. When the call came, the news was bad. Seligmann looked at his dad, and for the first time, he saw his father cry. He described his apprehension at the thought of having to call home to tell his mother, Kathy. "He dialed her number" and said, 'Mom, she picked me.'" He commented that "It was like the life was sucked out of her." He made her promise not to watch his arrest on television. But, the next day, Kathy found one of her other three sons sobbing in front of the television as he watched his brother being taken off to jail in handcuffs—in front of the whole world to see.

Seligmann had never been in any kind of trouble with the law before, and the article described the experience as somewhat surreal for him. "He found himself marveling at how cool the fingerprint machine was" and thought about studying for a Spanish exam, until he snapped back to reality. Thankfully, Seligmann spent only one hour behind bars. The media storm surrounding his family was so unrelenting that they decided to leave their New Jersey home to stay with friends in Connecticut. But Seligmann, knowing that he was innocent, told his mother, "What are we doing? I didn't do anything wrong. There's no reason to hide." The family returned home that same day to find that neighbors had tied yellow ribbons around the trees in support of their son.

After being forced to finish his spring semester at home, Seligmann's grades were good enough for him to make the athletic-conference honor roll. To keep busy, he spent most of his spare time as a volunteer worker at a soup kitchen, and he coached football at his old junior high school. One of his former coaches recommended that he read Rudyard Kipling's poem "If." Seligmann said he was glad that he took that advice, because sometimes reading the words of that poem is the only thing that helps him to sleep: "If you can trust yourself when all men doubt you. . . ."

He said that he keeps in touch with Evans and Finnerty and that the parents of the boys remain in close touch as well. Having already had plans to attend law school, Seligmann said that he now wants to become a criminal defense lawyer. He received a gift from his friends at Duke, his jersey and the nametag from his locker that reads, "READE SELIGMANN, DUKE BLUE DEVILS, #45." He put some things away in his basement, but hung his name on the wall. It's a tough reminder for him, "of a team and school that he misses . . . and of a past that is not yet behind him."

After the fact, when people are waiting for their criminal cases to be adjudicated, they often turn to activities that will help them look like worthwhile citizens in an effort to make a good impression on a judge. This is not the case for Seligmann. He is a young man who has always been involved in selfless and extremely worthwhile activities, just because it is the right thing to do.

According to an affidavit filed on June 21, 2006, by Philip Seligmann in support of his son's application to the court to decrease the amount of his bond, "Reade was recruited by every Ivy League school to play either football or lacrosse," and he was on the Atlantic Coast Conference (ACC) Honor Roll during his freshman year. Philip Seligmann went on to paint a picture of Reade that few parents can match:

> During his high school summers, Reade was a counselor for the Lacrosse Camp at his high school, Delbarton, as well as the Tri-State Lacrosse Program and the Princeton University Lacrosse Camp. At Delbarton, Reade was selected to participate in the Appalachia Project organized to send students to Appalachia to help the poor mountain children of eastern Kentucky. He was also selected by a panel of students and teachers at Delbarton during both his junior and senior years for the Deanery Program, which is a leadership position to encourage younger students to achieve high academic goals, participate in community service projects, and get involved in athletics. Reade was also a member of Bridges, a program at Delbarton where students go into some of the poorest neighborhoods of New York City at night to bring food and clothing to the homeless during especially bad weather.

Attached to the senior Seligmann's affidavit is documentation verifying his son's substantial achievements and extensive community service work. There are also pictures of Reade dressed in a Santa Claus costume and surrounded by children while he was part of the Appalachia Project. His Duke transcript is also included, which reflects that his overall grade point average at the school was 3.33 for grades posted prior to the spring 2006 semester. Also included with the affidavit is a letter of acceptance into the Appalachia Project and a certificate of appreciation for his participation in Bridges. Finally, there are letters of strong support from Delbarton written long before the alleged incident of March 13, 2006.

Reade Seligmann is simply an exceptional human being. Through campus interviews, I was able to find out that the guys on the lacrosse team affectionately called Reade "Mom." One person told me that "He was extremely on top of things and never wanted to get into trouble. He was always very careful about doing the right thing." I was told that Reade is driven, that he has a deep desire to accomplish things, and that he expects a lot from himself. He's very committed to doing well in school and on the field. Some individuals said that they were most impressed by the way that Reade dealt with the rape allegations. I heard that after Reade's room was searched and after he had turned himself in to police, he was able to maintain a sense of calm. This must have been enormously difficult considering what he and his teammates had already been enduring.

The words of a former fellow team member of Seligmann's say it all. On May 2, 2006, a Duke lacrosse player who wanted to remain anonymous had his face blacked out while he made a statement on abctv.com, expressing the isolation and persecution he and his team members felt after the allegations were made. He insisted that there was no rape and expressed his support for Coach Pressler and his team. The student said that "Duke University officials turned their backs on the team." He added that "From the get-go, we've only had each other to fall back on." The student stated what we have all come to learn: "We've been convicted in the media. Our university turned its back on us. . . . They didn't stand up for us. We feel neglected, and we feel that our loyalty to the university wasn't reciprocated." Hearing this saddened me, disturbed me, and caused me great pain. As a loyal alumnus who loves Duke, hearing his words simply broke my heart.

Speaking in reference to the reports that Coach Pressler had resigned, the team member commented that "He didn't resign. He was forced out. . . . The notion that he quit or resigned is ridiculous." Discussing the possibility of another indictment (only Finnerty and Seligmann had been indicted at this point), he said, "I just pray . . . that Nifong doesn't indict another innocent person. . . . We're all anxious, because even if it's not me, it's going to be somebody else who I care about."

He also had something to say about Nifong. "I wish he hadn't said the DNA was going to exclude innocent parties. Because, in our minds, we thought this was all going to come back negative and this is going to be over. So from our perspective, we thought this was going to be over, and from the community's perspective, they thought they were going to get three guilty parties. And neither came back."

A May 16, 2006, article on ESPN.go.com entitled "Duke Co-Captain Posts Bond, Released," reflects on Dave Evans's character. According to the article, Evans was an economics major at Duke before graduating on May 14, 2006, just one day before he was indicted. He attended Duke after graduating from the Landon School, a prep school outside of Washington DC where he played football and hockey and led his lacrosse team to a three-year record of 56–2. The article quotes the school's headmaster, David M. Armstrong, as calling Evans "an exemplary student and athlete" and added that "The allegations coming from Durham . . . are inconsistent with the character of the young man who attended our school." A fellow Duke student described Dave as the kind of guy that everyone feels comfortable around, very funny, great sense of humor, and very outgoing. People I spoke to said he has a way about him that makes people feel at ease. He's very personable, and while his sense of humor adds a kind of charm, he can also be very serious. I had that impression of him myself when I watched him speak to the media prior to turning himself in.

Collin, according to those who know him, has a gentle demeanor, is very polite, very respectful, laid back, and soft-spoken. I was also told that he is extremely bright and that he doesn't stress over things, that he is a "go with the flow" kind of guy. Friends mentioned that they found him to be very genuine, that he was the type of person who would hug you rather than shake your hand.

A July 1, 2006, *Newsday* article entitled "Duke Dad Says Evidence Clears Son" quotes Collin Finnerty's father, Kevin, saying that there is evidence that proves that it was "impossible" for his son to have committed the crimes for which he was charged. Some of this evidence includes "witnesses, commercial receipt(s), a dorm card, and cell phone records."

Finnerty said that Collin sailed through Chaminade, a private Catholic school in Mineola, New York, where he was on the honor roll and made it through four years without earning any demerits. He explained that Collin also sailed through something else, probably much more meaningful to him today than his prior credentials: he was given a lie detector test. The FBI expert who administered the exam is highly qualified and also trains other agents to give them. When the exam ended, the man told Finnerty's father, "This boy is innocent. He's telling the truth." Finnerty's mother, Mary Ellen, called the identification process used to allow Mangum to identify Evans, Finnerty, and Seligmann as "sort of a pin the tail on the donkey." Now that the facts have unraveled, it is apparent that that's just what it was. It was, in the worst of terms, a frame-up, a conspiracy that reaches from the very top of the ladder to the lowest rung. And part of what has helped the boys get through this very tragic ordeal was the ongoing and never-wavering support of their parents, family, teammates, and friends.

Last spring, after the media began reporting Mangum's allegations, I had an opportunity to visit with Emma Stevenson, a Duke student who was friends with many of the members of the lacrosse team. Emma, the daughter of my old friend and former teammate, Randy Stevenson, was passing through Nashville, and it afforded my wife Barbara, and me the opportunity to spend some time with her. My close friend Larry Saunders, who was the captain of our basketball team during our senior year, and his wife, Debbie, invited Barbara and me to have dinner with them and Emma at their home. During the course of the evening, the subject of the lacrosse case came up. Emma told us that the lacrosse players are not the "hooligans" that some had portrayed them to be in the media. She also told us something very interesting about Collin Finnerty. After Nifong had publicly stated that he was going to bring formal charges against some of the lacrosse players, everyone was waiting anxiously to see who the unlucky players would be. Emma and her friends at Duke sat around musing about who would be the least likely member of the lacrosse team to commit such a crime. They joked that Nifong would probably indict someone as unlikely as Collin Finnerty because Collin was one of the nicest guys on the team and one of the least likely to hurt anyone. They were shocked and dismayed when they later found out that Finnerty was, in fact, indicted. As it turned out, all three of the indicted boys were unlikely suspects for such outrageous accusations.

Apparently, all three boys are very unique in their own ways, but the one thing that everyone was in agreement about is this: they could never have committed the crimes that were alleged against them. One person said, "There was just no way. I had no doubt in my mind. I've even been around these guys when they were drinking and they were never like that." Another added, "There was absolutely no way that those three wonderful guys could have ever done anything that they have been accused of in this case." She added that she has enormous compassion for rape victims, but she said she has just as much compassion for Reade, Collin, and David, because there is obviously no rape victim in this case.

I've been told that the boys' families are extremely strong and supportive and dedicated to seeing that justice is served. That's the impression that I've been getting from everyone who has had any contact with the boys and their families, either before or after the allegations surfaced.

I am the father of three grown children myself, and I have had over thirty years of experience as a trial lawyer. That has provided me with a substantial amount of experience in evaluating people's credibility and human weaknesses. In investigating the Duke lacrosse case, I have seen nothing that remotely indicates that any one of the indicted players could have ever committed such a despicable act. They come from solid, supportive, and loving families, and they have demonstrated their willingness and ability to grow into fine, responsible young men. They are not just young men who have achieved much scholastically and on the athletic field, they are kind-natured young men of strong moral character.

Although those on their side have not been as outwardly vocal as the hate groups, I have found that there is an enormous amount of support for these boys, and those individuals have been doing everything they can to turn the situation around. A small example of that support is found at www.ipetitions.com on a page called "Support Reade," where a petition was created on behalf of Reade Seligmann. The text of the petition reads, "Anyone who has ever known Reade Seligmann can attest to the fact that he is an honest, caring, gentle person and friend. By signing this petition, we are showing our support for Reade, stating our belief in his innocence, and standing up for his strong character." As I am writing this, there are over nineteen hundred signatures on the petition along with encouraging comments from those who signed, including the following:

Petitioner #5, Brooke Jandl—"He's the most amazing person I have ever met, with the biggest heart. He is full of love and considers everyone before himself. Everyone that knows Reade loves him."

Petitioner #22, Katelin Sensibaugh—"Reade we love you!!!!!!!!"

Petitioner #41, Lindsay Baker-Baum—"Reade is a great guy and there is no way that these allegations are true. I fully support him. He is a great friend, and one of the least violent people I know. He's always been the one to break up a fight, not instigate it. If there's anything I can do to help, let me know."

Petitioner #5, Brooke Jandl, added, "I just want to say that although I have already commented on how amazing Reade is, I wanted to state my overwhelming support for Collin Finnerty also. I can attest to his wonderful and fun-loving demeanor, and will guarantee his innocence as well. Thanks."

Petitioner #112, Rob Wellington—"Reade is way too good of a person for this."

Petitioner #113, Aaina Agarwal—"Reade and Colin are both amazing gentle souls who are innocent beyond a doubt. Honorable, trustworthy, and full of love for other people . . . please support them and support the truth!"

Petitioner #293, Neil Murphy—"We have your back Reade."

Petitioner #618, Charlie Ellinwood—"I went to school with Reade for a year and it is painfully obvious that he'd never do what he's being accused of. Moreover, the Durham D.A. and the president of Duke should apologize to the lacrosse team and Mike Pressler for their cancelled season."

Petitioner #717, Stephany Johnson—"God Bless you and keep you strong. Know that millions of people all over the country are supporting you, Collin, and Dave! If there is a way for our family to donate money for your defense costs please contact us immediately. You are a good kid and so are your teammates. Hang On, Be Strong. Love Mark, Stephany, and Shea Johnson."

Petitioner # 1759, Charlie Hatfield—"Absolute travesty. We need to be sure that after these kids are acquitted or the case is dropped, that the D.A. loses his job and is disgraced in front of this nation. Pennyless and homeless is too good for him."

Petitioner #1901, 41 (who just might be Ryan Mcfadyen because #41 is his lacrosse jersey number)—"innocent! I love ya baby."

The most touching words of all were from Petitioner #1556, Kathy Seligmann, Reade's mother, who wrote, "Thank you all for your kind words of love and support for my son. You cannot imagine how much it means to not only Reade, but to our entire family. You have helped to restore our faith in human kindness. We are forever grateful."

On October 15, 2006, Ed Bradley from *60 Minutes* interviewed the three indicted lacrosse players. During that interview, Evans commented that "[Mangum] has destroyed everything I worked for in my life. She's put it on hold. She's destroyed two other families, and she's brought shame on a great university. And, worst of all, she's split apart a community and a nation on facts that just didn't happen and a lie that never should have been told."

Collin Finnerty also spoke to Bradley. He was hard-pressed to understand why this had happened to him. "I never expected anything even close to that happening. I never expected anyone to get indicted, let alone myself," he said.

Seligmann added, "Your whole life you try to . . . stay on the right path and to do the right things. And someone can come along and take it all away. . . . Just by pointing their finger. That's all it takes."

What has now become increasingly obvious to most observers is that Mangum's allegations are totally false, and that she pointed her finger at three randomly chosen, innocent young men. I can only imagine what all of the members of the Duke lacrosse team must have been thinking during the days just before the indictments were announced. They knew that nothing happened at the party that would remotely support any allegations of assault, much less rape, and they knew that they were all innocent of any such charges. Mangum was supposedly going to pick three of them who would then be indicted for these serious crimes, but they had no idea which three it would be. It must have felt like they were playing a dangerous game of Russian roulette—who would be the unlucky ones? What a nightmare!

9

THE SILENCE OF
WHITE RAPE

As so often happens in situations where crimes have been alleged, there were many people who had no particular connection to the Duke family that came forward in support of the accuser. As early as April 15, 2006, only one month after Mangum accused the team members of rape, and prior to Evans, Finnerty, and Seligmann's indictments, the Reverend Jesse Jackson announced that his Rainbow/PUSH Coalition would pay Mangum's college tuition. In adding that he believed that there was enough circumstantial evidence to indicate that something had happened to the woman, he made it clear that he had already determined that the lacrosse team members were guilty.

In keeping with tradition, on May 1, 2006, approximately thirty members of the New Black Panthers Party (NBPP), including Malik Zulu Shabazz, national chairman for the group, came to Durham to hold a rally in support of Mangum. At this point, Finnerty and Seligmann had been indicted, but Evans had not. Shabazz has stated that while he was in town, he was allowed to review Nifong's evidence in the case against the boys, a move that I, as an attorney, find quite disturbing on Nifong's part, if true. Shabazz is not a member of the Durham community, nor is he personally involved with the victim. He did, however, have one thing that made him relevant to Nifong: his influence in certain segments of the black community, the support that was critical to Nifong's chances of winning the upcoming election. So it wouldn't be surprising to me, especially considering what I have learned about Nifong to date, if he would discuss the evidence in his case with Shabazz while refusing to see what the defense attorneys had vehemently tried to share with him. I suppose if Nifong didn't see it, nobody can accuse him of knowing about it and ignoring it.

Shabazz and his group rallied near the Duke campus. While chants of "Black power, black power" were heard throughout the crowd, a member of the NBPP told the audience that he was not there to play the race card. "You with all the cameras, your forefathers been playing race cards for the past four hundred and fifty years," he called out to them. Another member said, "We will defend our black women. The New Black Panther Party and black men is [sic] not going to stand by, idly by, and let our black women be raped." And as Shabazz yelled out, "How do you find the two defendants in this case?" members of the crowd shouted back, "Guilty." It is chilling for me to even imagine this scene actually taking place.

It is odd that they claimed to not be playing the race card while shouting "Black power" and consistently referring to Mangum as "black." A glance at their organization's "10 Point Program" makes it obvious that their fundamental principles are all about playing the race card. (For more information, go to www.newblackpanther.com.)

They espouse the belief that "the white man has kept us deaf, dumb and blind, and used every 'dirty trick' in the book to stand in the way of our freedom and independence." They advocate on behalf of blacks for "tax exemption," "reparations," "education for our people that exposes the true nature of this devilish and decadent American society," and "exemption from the military service." Their call to action includes uniting all black people to form an "African United Front" and "arming themselves for self-defense." They demand "that all Black People and people of color should be released from the many jails and prisons because they have not received a fair and impartial trial." So, when they show up in groups and hold demonstrations where they make demands that they insist black people are entitled to, for no other purpose than that they are black, how can anyone assume that the "race card" is not at issue? The mere fact that Mangum is black and Evans, Finnerty, and Seligmann are white was what must have motivated them to travel to North Carolina for their demonstration of white hate.

After Duke University police refused to allow them to rally on campus, citing that it was exam week, the demonstrators headed to 610 North Buchanan Boulevard. I can only imagine what the scene must have been like for neighbors of the small, white, abandoned house when members of the NBPP began congregating outside of their homes. There was no way to know what they were capable of doing considering their history of threatening violence and their reputation for anti-Semitic slander.

According to the Web site of the Anti-Defamation League (www.adl.org), the New Black Panther Party is the "largest organized anti-Semitic and racist black militant group in America" and its symbol, a "leaping black panther superimposed over a green Africa on a red circle," signifies hate. The site describes the group's ideology as "a mix of black nationalism, Pan-Africanism, and anti-white, anti-Semitic bigotry." Also noted is that the group "organize[s] demonstrations across the country that blend inflammatory bigotry with calls for black empowerment and civil rights."

Additionally, the Southern Poverty Law Center (www.splcenter.org), well-known for its commitment to fighting against all forms of discrimination, lists the NBPP on its Web site as an "active U.S. hate group."

And there they were, standing in the streets of Durham, North Carolina, calling for action to seize justice for one of their own. They made several demands, including that the two currently charged players, Collin Finnerty and Reade Seligmann, be sent to prison and that all those who attended the party at 610 North Buchanan be expelled from school.

The publicity surrounding the alleged rape was probably the biggest draw for the NBPP, because it certainly wasn't merely about the rape of a human being. I've tried to find any articles detailing situations where the group was seen chanting outside of the homes of alleged black rapists. But I have been unable to find any. The only conclusion I can come to is that, just like the Group of 88, this was nothing more than an agenda-driven gathering for the purpose of furthering the goals of the NBPP by using the poor, black "victim," Mangum. And yes, in spite of all she has claimed, Mangum can be viewed as a victim in some respects. She was used and victimized by Nifong, the Group of 88, the NBPP, and even the NAACP, as you will read shortly. She was used for the selfish motives of those and so many others who apparently didn't give a thought to her at all. For the same reasons that they all crucified the boys, they martyred Mangum.

Mangum is obviously a very troubled person. Her history speaks for itself. She has made false rape allegations against others in the past, and she has a pretty extensive criminal record. In the early morning hours of March 14, 2006, she awakened from what may have been a drunken stupor and was confronted by a nurse who asked her if she had been raped. It is quite likely that she was just trying to avoid being thrown into the drunk tank when she answered yes. The events that followed are what caused the situation to explode onto the national scene and grow totally out of control. In the process, a series of inconsistent and false statements by Mangum dug her into a hole from which she will not be able to emerge.

In a normal situation of this type, her claim of rape would be followed by an investigation by honest policemen and/or a competent prosecutor who would then evaluate the case and decide whether to proceed with it. Based on the facts of this case, it should have been tossed on the very first day! Had that occurred, it would have saved Mangum from her own actions. The case would not have progressed any further, and we would have avoided all the mess that followed. But the boys were deemed criminals and Mangum was the victim of opportunity, and then the self-proclaimed vigilantes came out of the woodwork to shout their attacks in order to advance their own agendas.

In spite of all that has come to light, I have to wonder why the focus in this case has so consistently been trained on the alleged horrors acted out by the lacrosse players and the need for punishment and change on their part. They hired the women, and the women willingly went to their house to dance for them. And while everyone was busy sorting out which message they would use to condemn the boys, they missed the real tragedy. Nobody seemed to notice that the only message circulating was about the boys' "whiteness," "privilege," and "guilt."

If we have learned anything from this story, it's that this whole sordid affair should have, among other things, sent a clear message to *women* that there are situations that they should avoid, especially ones where they may be putting themselves at risk. I would venture to say that dancing naked for a group of guys who have been drinking is not a good choice, just as underage drinking and hiring strippers for a party are not good choices. But the messages that were being publicized as well as shared behind the closed door meetings at Duke were nothing more than counterproductive, McCarthy-like examples of racism and mass hysteria. This atmosphere incited throngs of lacrosse team bashers to take out incendiary ads and post messages on blogs and Web sites, some for sport and some to further their own agendas.

The NAACP has an interesting, yet thoroughly inaccurate history of the lacrosse case posted on its site. (See http://www.naacp ncnetwork.org/Publicity/768). I recognized some of their erroneous blunders as information that had been circulating on the Internet, but other statements also suggested that they weren't too concerned about getting to the truth. The author of the page entitled "Duke Lacrosse Update: Crimes and Torts committed by Duke Lacrosse Team Players on 3/13 and 3/14 as Reported in the press, mainly from the Three Players' Defense Attorneys" referred to David Evans as "Dan" and stated in paragraph ten that Evans and the other team captains "made a common plan to trick two female dancers to come to a party unescorted," and that "the Captains, including Defendant Evans, knew it was the policy . . . to send a body guard with a female dancer if [there were] more than 10–15 males in attendance." The organization presumably posted that because it has been alleged that the boys told the escort service that they were having a bachelor party with less than ten to fifteen people present. If Flannery had, in fact, said he was having a bachelor party, it might have been due to his embarrassment at having never hired a stripper before. And he may have felt uncomfortable admitting that he was hiring the women for a team gathering, when it is common knowledge that bachelor parties routinely have strippers as entertainment.

Rather than focusing on the escort service's own lack of safety verification procedures regarding where they send their "employees" to perform, the NAACP's site accused the boys of pulling a fast one on the escort service. The implication is that the boys were trying to lure the women to the party without their bodyguards. The reasonable inference one could then make is that the boys specifically hired the strippers for the purpose of raping one of them. Of course, that is an absurd assumption, but I can't think of what else they could be implying.

Escort services apparently hire out women every day to do all sorts of illicit things without any regard for their health or safety. They also book them on several dates in short periods of time. Although it isn't clear whether Mangum's appointments were always booked by an escort service, the following statement by Mangum's driver makes it clear that these women aren't too concerned about where they go and with whom they end up.

On April 6, 2006, Mangum's driver, Jarriel Johnson, gave a written statement to police. He said that Mangum had called him on March 10, 2006, and requested that he drive her to a Holiday Inn Express. He picked her up at approximately 1:50 p.m. and dropped her at the hotel at around 2:20 p.m. He returned to pick her up at around 2:50 p.m.

On March 11, 2006, between 11:00 p.m. and 12:00 a.m., Mangum asked Johnson to drive her to a club, and he remained in the car while she went inside. At 2:00 a.m., Johnson went into the club to find her, and she asked to stay for another hour. She then prolonged her stay until 4:30 a.m. At that time, Mangum told Johnson that she had a job at the Millenium Hotel. He drove her there at 5:15 a.m., and she went inside while he remained in the car. She returned at 6:15 a.m. and he drove her to her parents' house.

At approximately 2:00 p.m. that same day, March 12, Mangum again called Johnson for another ride for later that night. He picked her up at approximately 5:30 p.m., and they drove around until sometime between 8:00 p.m. and 9:00 p.m., when Mangum asked him to drive her to find some guy. When they didn't find him, they got a hotel room to wait to see if he called, and they then had sexual intercourse.

Johnson left, and at around 11:00 a.m. on March 13, 2006, Mangum called him to pick her up. When he arrived back at the hotel, Mangum was "with an older gentleman" who "want[ed] to see her perform." Johnson waited outside for her. Mangum called him later to tell him that she had a job at a bachelor party that night and asked him for a ride. He wasn't able to take her, so she told him her boyfriend, Brian, would take her.

At approximately 1:30 a.m. on March 14, Johnson received a call from the woman who books Mangum's jobs asking if he was her driver that night and he responded that he wasn't.

Based on that statement alone, it's not surprising that after Mangum claimed that the Duke lacrosse players had raped her, DNA test results revealed that she did, in fact, have the DNA of several different men inside of her, none of it belonging to Duke lacrosse players.

Getting back to the NAACP's assertion that escort services could be "tricked" into sending women to unsafe places, this idea is beyond ludicrous. Even more ridiculous is the automatic assumption that a woman would be safe dancing half-naked at a party in front of even "10–15" men without having a bodyguard present.

The plain truth is that the lacrosse captains had no idea what the policies of the escort service were, because they had never before hired an exotic dancer, which is why Dan Flannery had to spend time googling one up on the Internet. He was able to recreate his search for the police and for Bob Ekstrand, as well. It must have been apparent to the person who answered the phone at the escort service that Flannery was a first-time caller due to the type of exchange they had. Bob told me that after Flannery requested two dancers, the person asked him what he wanted. Flannery's naïve response was, "What do you mean?" Then Flannery was offered a smorgasbord of women from which to choose; white, black, brunette, blonde, thin, heavy, tall, short, until he requested females who were "thin, white, and as pretty as you have." He finally agreed to hire the two women the person on the phone offered him: a Latino female and a woman with brown hair and blonde highlights. Clearly, if anyone was tricked, it was the lacrosse players who were not expecting the two African American women that the escort service sent.

Another incorrect statement can be found in paragraph eleven on the NAACP page that states that Devon Sherwood, the only African American team member, was at the party but left before the dancers arrived. As mentioned in an earlier chapter, on October 31, 2006,

Sherwood stated on ABC's *Good Morning America* that he stayed for the dance and then left with some of the other players because, as the others would acknowledge and the pictures clearly demonstrate, "It was kind of boring. . . .We were just sitting around. And there was nothing to it. It was very boring." The pictures clearly show a group of young men doing just as Sherwood described, "sitting around" looking bored. No expressions of excitement on their faces. Nobody seemed interested in what was going on. It is inconceivable that in a mere few minutes, they would have all gone into an alcohol-induced state of delirium and started violently raping Mangum.

Aside from the incorrect facts on the NAACP's site, there are also omissions that distort the truth. In the timeline of the events of March 13, the details are conveniently spun in favor of Mangum by leaving out documented items of interest that would fill in the gaps and significantly change the NAACP's version. For example, in paragraph forty-three, there is a description of Mangum's condition while she was still in Roberts's car in Kroger's parking lot during the early morning hours of March 14, 2006. It states in part, "When [the police officer] got no response when he talked loudly to her, he pressured her wrists to try to get her out of the car. Ms. M. grabbed the parking brake, and struggled to stay in the car. When he got Ms. M. out, she collapsed on the pavement." Omitted is the statement from the police report that when Mangum appeared unresponsive, the officer waved smelling salts under her nose and she started breathing out of her mouth, which indicated to him that she was feigning unconsciousness.

Paragraph seventy-six is also revealing: In explaining why the defense filed a change of venue motion, the site said, "[The defense is] worried the egregious racism of some of the players will affect a Durham jury, just as it has affected all people of good will who are outraged by the arrogant, entitled behavior of these men, whether or not three men physically assaulted an obviously almost comatose woman." In other words, the boys are guilty of something, no matter what did or did not happen to Mangum. And it's not enough that all of the evidence weighs heavily in their favor or that they are dedicated, hard-working, worthwhile individuals; their incorrectly perceived "egregious racism" and "arrogant, entitled behavior" would be all that's necessary for a Durham jury to convict them. That alone is a strong and compelling enough basis for a change of venue.

I can only imagine what the courthouse steps would look like with people like these or the New Black Panthers lining them. This is not really about the lacrosse team. This is about a deep-seated hatred and grief for a history of past suffering that is very real to African Americans, and it would not be inaccurate to say that much of their past suffering was caused by white people. But some African Americans have redirected their hatred, taking it out of the historical realm and into today's world in their quest to punish innocent people who had nothing to do with the suffering of their ancestors.

In January 2007, Rev. Dr. William Barber, the president of the NAACP's North Carolina chapter, stated to ESPN, "We sincerely believe that the high level of public scrutiny and controversy involved in this matter is unwarranted and threatens to pervert the truth-finding process." However, the Web site's damning statements against the Duke Three remain.

The NAACP has drawn some criticism for the manner in which they have responded to this case. Professor Coleman stated to me, "They should have been outraged that the prosecutor was treating these students this way, because you've got black people that get cheated all the time and they should be opposed to this kind of thing whenever it happens, because if he's doing it to these guys, you don't even want to think about what he's doing to the people who are poor." Coleman saw the NAACP's actions as payback for what African Americans have endured at the hands of racists. He felt that they were, in effect, applauding what Nifong was doing to these students given the publicity and the spotlight. He continued, "The reason we need to criticize this behavior is because if the system isn't working at this level, it's not working anywhere. And a lot of people are getting hurt. All of us should be concerned. That's the point here. All of us ought to be champions and opposed to this kind of thing. And it doesn't matter whether we think these kids are whatever we think they are."

My cowriter, Stephanie Good, recounts hearing a pastor give a sermon that touched on issues of privilege, class, and race. Those three things, he stated, intertwine to influence people's perception of others. He explained that privileged people are viewed as those who think they are better than most and that other people resent them for it. She was following his words contentedly until he began saying things like, "Golf is the white man's sport," "Women are generally too intimidated by privileged men to interrupt them," and "People are born into privilege and cannot achieve it on their own." He also commented several times that he is a man who is privileged. Stephanie started wondering where he was going with these comments because they really didn't hit home with her at all. It was early in the morning at the time. In fact, it was the day the clocks were turned ahead, so it was very early. She had been in somewhat of a comfortable daze, glancing out the window while listening to the melodic voice of the pastor, until she heard those comments. She was immediately taken aback.

After the sermon, Stephanie approached the pastor to ask him about some of his statements. She told him that she was especially interested in his sermon because of our research regarding the Duke lacrosse allegations. She explained how the appearance of privilege and class in the case had been a big factor in turning the public perception against the lacrosse players and that people had been displaying a lynch-mob attitude toward the boys simply because they are white athletes at Duke University. She told him how unfairly the boys had been treated. His reaction floored her. He said that the perception was correct and that it's okay for the boys to suffer the consequences they are enduring because, after all, historically African Americans have suffered that way also. She responded with, "This isn't about history. The case is about today and the boys are innocent." He broke out into a pompous grin and said, "No matter, it's only fair that they should suffer the way that blacks have." Surprisingly, the pastor was white. Stephanie felt as though she was talking to a member of the Group of 88.

It is disappointing to hear something like that, especially from a pastor. I am not a pastor, but I have read the Bible, and I do not believe that this view is consistent with what scripture teaches us on the subject. Some white people seem to have a sense of guilt about white people's history of racism toward black people. That makes no sense to me unless you have done something for which you should feel guilty. It is highly unfortunate that acts of racism have been committed in the past, and it is detestable that some forms of racism still exist today. Racism is despicable in any form, and it has no place in our society. However, while the acts of racism committed by others disgust me, I do not personally feel guilty about them, because I am not a racist and have never been one. Furthermore, I certainly do not subscribe to the philosophy that we should punish somebody who is not guilty of any wrongdoing as a form of payback for the wrongful actions that may have been committed by others.

The pastor that Stephanie spoke to must have had a distorted sense of reality. I wonder if he would have still had the same opinion had his son been one of the boys on the lacrosse team.

The NAACP's Web site displays a similar tendency to distort reality. The facts of the lacrosse case as noted there are twisted to suit the agendas of those who wrote them. I believe that these authors deliberately made the issue one of race, white against black and black dominated by white, in order to pummel it into the ground to make some headway for their cause. They had a lot of company. During those first several months after Mangum's allegations were made, more people were heard condemning the boys than supporting them. And along with their comments, there was speculation that if the dancers were not African American, the night would have gone differently.

I mentioned earlier a comment made by the Associate Professor of African-American Studies, Mark Anthony Neal, who while being interviewed by ESPN on April 3, 2006, said, "For me, this is not simply a case of sexual violence or just a case of racism. It's a case of racialized sexual violence, meaning if it had been a white woman in that room, it would not have gone down the same way." I added the following comment shortly thereafter in reference to Neal's statement: "I do believe that this is an issue of race, because if the situation involved all black kids, all white kids, or a white victim and a black perpetrator, I doubt whether we would be hearing the multitude of racial slurs that Finnerty, Seligmann, and Evans have received merely because they are white." I continued with, "I know that to be the case" and said I would expand on that later. It is time for me to do just that.

Nearly a year after the Duke lacrosse allegations were made, another rape involving Duke students took place. A party was thrown on February 11, 2007, by members of the fraternity Phi Beta Sigma at an off-campus house in Durham where one fraternity member lived with three other Duke students. After the alleged incident, they were moved into campus housing by Duke administrators. An eighteen-year-old female claimed that during the party attended by approximately fifty people, she was raped in the bathroom. The victim and some of the partygoers were able to assist police in identifying the suspect and he was arrested. At first glance, one feels relief that a suspect has been apprehended. And it is comforting to know that Duke administrators cared so much about their students that they moved them to safety. But, look again, because the picture is going to become quite distorted. The two alleged rapes have parallels, but there is a point at which the lines merge, then cross over, and change directions. It is the point of injustice, and the change in direction is very sharp.

It has been a few months since the more recent rape allegations were made, and to date, we have not seen one demonstration, one potbanger, one wanted poster, or any calls to action from the Group of 88. The fraternity has not been shut down or suspended. The New Black Panthers have not come to march on Durham, and unless I've missed it, neither Jesse Jackson nor anyone else is offering any scholarships to the victim. I also haven't found anything damning about the suspect on the NAACP's site. While it is possible that something will appear on there before this book is released, I highly doubt it. Nobody is carrying threatening banners or chanting "guilty" in front of the house where the alleged rape took place. Bullhorns are nowhere to be found, and no one is demanding justice and crying out for the poor repressed victim of a racist society that caters to the white man. There are no "we know you know" articles, and no demands for expulsions or more arrests. There is nobody to thank for "not waiting," because everybody is waiting. No committees are being formed at Duke. The campus and surrounding community is silent—this time. The district attorney is silent—this time. They are doing what they should be doing—allowing due process to run its course. I'd like to believe that this change of heart is all due to the lessons that were learned from the lacrosse incident. I'd *like* to think so. But I doubt that the mistakes that were made in the lacrosse case have any bearing on why there are such glaring differences this time around. Here's why:

Unlike Mangum, the new victim is white.

Unlike Mangum, the new victim is a student at Duke University.

Unlike the Duke Three, the suspect, Michael Jermaine Burch, is black.

Unlike the Duke Three, the suspect does not attend Duke.

Unlike the Duke lacrosse team, Phi Beta Sigma is known for having primarily black members.

Amazingly, there are additional differences that create a stark contrast between the two cases. Unlike the Duke lacrosse house, there were drugs and weapons found at the house where the new rape allegedly occurred.

Unlike the lacrosse team's unforgivable act of serving up alcohol to underage students, nobody is raising the same hell over the possession of weapons and the possession and use of illegal drugs at the party where the new rape occurred.

Unlike the Duke Three, the suspect in the new rape case was assigned a $50,000 bail, not $400,000.

In essence, the big difference, the one that counted the most for those who used Mangum's accusations to further their causes, is this: Unlike the allegations involving the Duke Three, this new arrest involved a "white rape."

So then, what is the real lesson here?

A black girl alleges rape and the convergence of hate, outrage, and vengeance is swift and unyielding. The pressure from hate groups, the politically correct media, and people in authority with the wrong agendas cause the walls of prejudice to befall a group of college kids who have absolutely no culpability at all. They were offered no protection, no safe place in which to hide. Unlike the "white rape," there is no concern for their safety.

A black girl alleges rape and forty-six members of the Duke lacrosse team are ordered to submit to DNA testing and have their mug shots taken; the nationally ranked lacrosse team sits out the rest of its season; an award-winning coach is fired; three young men's futures are ripped out from under them; families are devastated and forced to strain their finances to pay for their sons' legal fees; and Duke University's administration fails to properly support these young men during their darkest hours because it allowed a more vocal minority group within its faculty to intimidate it. And even after Mangum's case began to unravel and it became more and more obvious that it was based on lies, their situation was treated no differently. Where was the outrage *for* them? Where were the demonstrations?

A black girl alleges rape, and the Duke administration caves in to the demands of a handful of people who shout the loudest.

But when a white girl alleges rape, there is silence. To the outside world, it is as though it never happened, because to Nifong, the pot-banging demonstrators, the righteously indignant Group of 88, the NAACP, the New Black Panthers, Jesse Jackson, Houston Baker, Karla Holloway, and the dozens of others who made their racist and prejudicial voices heard; this rape doesn't count the same way. It doesn't further their agendas. It doesn't give them a soapbox to stand on. If the white man can't be the scapegoat or the sacrificial lamb, then what's the point?

There were people who said the issue in the lacrosse case was one of rape, not race. *Where are they now?* They were so passionate about their cause, so socially responsible, only wanting to right society's wrongs. Isn't it equally wrong for a white girl to be raped? Are the hate groups pulling back because the truth is they only "hate" when it comes to white people? After all, it's not politically correct to talk badly about African Americans, not if you're white. However, it would appear that racial antagonism and sexual exploitation are acceptable only if they are aimed at white people. Fling it at black people and you have a whole different issue brewing. Or do the hate groups and so-called social action committees remain quiet out of fear? After all, imagine what groups like the New Black Panthers would do if a mob of white people descended on Michael Jermaine Burch's house for allegedly raping a white girl in the bathroom at a Duke fraternity party?

There is one more side to all of this in addition to the issue of "whiteness." There is Nifong. He's not running for election now. That train has already pulled into the station. He's not out there selling a bill of goods to the black caucus. He doesn't need their votes now. He won his election. In March 2006, he had a lot of influence. He was high on his game when nobody doubted his word or doubted his motives when he was using people to get what he wanted. He did have a little help from his friends though. There were those whom he convinced right out in the open to help him, but some might suggest that he may have had a little influence on people who didn't publicly acknowledge their admiration for him and his hold over them. For instance, in the November election, Nifong faced opposition from an attorney, County Commissioner Lewis Cheek, an Independent who said if elected, he would not serve. Instead, he would leave it up to Governor Easley to appoint a replacement. Citing the reason that he did not want to harm his newly formed legal practice, Cheek urged others to vote for him in a show of disapproval for Nifong. Nifong's other challenger was a Republican write-in candidate, Steve Monks, who Wes Covington told me ended up splitting the votes that would have gone against Nifong.

Apparently, Nifong also had some indirect support from the Duke University administration. In the fall, as the tide was turning in favor of the boys, some Dukies formed "Duke Students for an Ethical Durham" to encourage their classmates to exercise their right to vote as Durham residents. The group endorsed Cheek. However, when they attempted to register voters outside of the Duke football stadium, the university shut them down. The election was coming up and the group, students who were basically fed up with Nifong's "politics," wanted to set up a voter registration booth on the Saturday of a home football game because a lot of students would be there. Professor Steve Baldwin told me that, "The idea was to get the students to register so they would vote against Nifong and he'd be gone. Of course, they assumed that if they could get Duke undergraduates to vote, they would support their classmates [the Duke Three]." He added, "That's a smart thing to do. But they didn't say this at the booth; it was just a booth to register to vote." Baldwin continued, "One of the deans came by and shut it down, saying 'We just don't want you doing this. We think it's a distraction.' Think about it. This is an official university policy discouraging young Americans from registering to vote." Baldwin was obviously disturbed at the university's actions. "It's outrageous. It was like the South in the '60s," he said.

Ironically, while Duke students weren't allowed to exercise their constitutional right to register to vote on school grounds, Duke officials had no problem allowing the militant New Black Panthers to congregate in the university parking lot prior to holding their hate-filled May 2006 demonstrations.

As a Duke alumnus, I was outraged. I couldn't help but wonder who was at the helm of such a despicable act. The student organization had been actively endorsing an opponent of Nifong's. It seemed more than a coincidence that they were stopped from registering voters in an environment where many of the young people would have most likely voted in a show of support for their three fellow students who had been abused by Nifong. Interfering with the registration process was a signal to many people that Duke administrators and members of the faculty were supporting Nifong in his quest to win the election, and even worse, to win a conviction. By the time of this incident, it had already become clear that something was amiss in the lacrosse case. It seems inconceivable that the very people whose job it was to watch over the students would endorse a man who had done everything in his power to stomp on the constitutional rights of Evans, Finnerty, Seligmann, and the rest of the lacrosse team.

Nifong did prevail in the November election with approximately 49 percent of the vote. However, according to K.C. Johnson's Durham-in-Wonderland blog, Nifong pulled in somewhere between 90 to 95 percent of the black vote. Obviously, without such an unusually high percentage of the black vote, Nifong would have fallen short and lost the election. After he won, Nifong was quoted as saying, "I really felt like I was the best candidate all along. I am satisfied I did the case as it should be done. I am satisfied I did the campaign as it should be done."

Nifong won on the backs of the Duke Three and with the support (either intended or unwitting) of numerous individuals, including Duke University administrators and faculty members, those belonging to hate groups, and local members of the African American community. But, even after achieving his goal of being elected Durham County District Attorney, Nifong continued on with his shameful campaign to prosecute the Duke Three.

10

**THE END
IS NEAR**

Durham was quieting down, and people had begun seeing the shifting tide from absolute guilt to total vindication for the Duke Three. By now, it was fairly easy to recognize that something was rotten in Durham, and it certainly wasn't the lacrosse team. Mangum had changed her story again, nine months after offering her first versions. Nifong dropped the rape charges against the boys, which in effect, impeached Mangum's credibility, even though he would never admit that. And it was clear that the list of Nifong supporters had dwindled down significantly, if there were any left at all besides the stalwarts who simply refused to admit that they were wrong. The evidence against Nifong was very strong and much too damning to even question. He had done just about everything wrong in this case, including the following: condemning the lacrosse team in the press, ignoring alibis, refusing to give polygraph tests, disregarding DNA evidence and failing to stand by his office's promise that it would be used to rule out innocent persons, conspiring to hide exculpatory evidence from the defendants, refusing to acknowledge the numerous discrepancies in Mangum's statements and photo identifications, lying to the court, and continuing on with the charges even after realizing that he could no longer pursue Mangum's claims of rape. With Nifong finally off the case, maybe there would finally be some justice and relief for Evans, Finnerty, and Seligmann!

On January 14, 2007, Dr. Brian Meehan, Nifong's expert hired to examine the DNA samples acquired from the forty-six Duke lacrosse team members, the premises at 610 North Buchanan, and Mangum, was interviewed by *60 Minutes* correspondent Leslie Stahl. During the broadcast, we all watched as Meehan admitted publicly that he had made a "big error" by omitting from his report the crucial information that the only DNA found on Mangum came from several men who were not on the Duke lacrosse team. As discussed earlier, the evidence was exculpatory and essential to the Duke Three's defense. While claiming that he had never done anything like that before, he also acknowledged that he had informed Nifong of those results in April 2006, at which time Nifong and he agreed that the DNA report would be limited to only "positive" results between the lacrosse players and Mangum. Those who had not followed the case closely were astounded by what they saw as a new bombshell. Little did they know that it was just the tip of a very huge, melting iceberg.

By now, with the rape charges dropped and Nifong off the case, all of the pieces of the puzzle were finally starting to fit together and the crusade against the boys wasn't as much fun anymore for those who had been on the attack. Even the members of the Group of 88 were apparently trying to justify their actions. They lost a few members and changed their name to "Concerned Duke Faculty" and made an attempt to take back what they had said in their April 2006 ad by, well, denying that it meant what it said. On January 16, 2007, in an open letter on their Web site, they claimed that "[They] reject all attempts to try the case outside the courts, and stand firmly by the principle of the presumption of innocence." In regard to their original ad, they also now insist that "The ad thanked 'the students speaking individually and . . . the protesters making collective noise.'" However, they added a disclaimer, "We do not endorse every demonstration that took place at the time."

Lest you forget what their ad actually said, I will remind you: "We're turning up the volume in a moment when some of the most vulnerable among us are being asked to quiet down while we wait. To the students speaking individually and to the protestors making collective noise, thank you for not waiting and for making yourselves heard." Nowhere does their ad specify that they are only thanking certain demonstrators. Nowhere does it differentiate between the demonstrations so as to clarify which ones they approved of and which they were not endorsing. I also do not recall any rallies or demonstrations during that time that were not negative attacks on the boys. So what difference would it make if we knew which ones they supported?

This is what happens when you jump on a bandwagon and the wheels start getting stuck in the mud. You try to go backwards, a term referred to in situations like this as backpedaling. Then you have everyone pile into the wagon and encourage them to rock back and forth in order to loosen the wheels and continue moving forward. But that mud, that "murky pool of agenda-filled mud" that they were so caught up in last spring, is not so easy to climb out of once they're in it up to their neck. However, they are certainly trying.

A recent article appeared in Duke University's newspaper, *The Chronicle*, entitled "They Found 88 Problems, and the Dancer Was Just One." I read through it carefully, three times to be exact, in order to make sure that I wasn't misinterpreting its content. I explain this because much of what was written involved the Group of 88's original ad from last spring. But this article was about how the group has apparently become a band of tortured souls since their ad first appeared and was so terribly misconstrued—according to them. Those members of the group who were quoted in the recent article still stood by their ad, but only after appending a few more disclaimers to it. One said that they "had a short window to add their signatures to the document. 'I had to tell them in six hours if I wanted to sign it,'" claimed Diane Nelson, associate professor of cultural anthropology, and one of the original ad's signatories. What she seemed to be saying was that she had to make a "rush-to-judgment" decision (how ironic!) to sign the ad or the window would have closed and forever left her— what—flailing in space? Lost in time? Ejected from the Group? The other question that I have is this: Was she not capable of reading that short ad in six hours and recognizing right then and there that it was a statement that at least implied that the members of the lacrosse team were guilty of the allegations? I certainly was! The majority of other people who read it were able to make an immediate decision about the ad's intent, as well. After all, according to the article, "after the blogosphere picked up on the ad, professors each received hundreds of anonymous mass e-mails, most of which were racist, misogynistic and deeply personal profanity-laced diatribes. E-mail campaigns were targeted at specific, mostly African-American individuals, who received thousands of 'ugly' e-mails."

"Another associate professor of cultural anthropology and chair of the Arts and Sciences Council" who signed the ad was Lee Baker, who stated, "I, for one, did not think through all of the unintended consequences, nor did I believe almost a year later it would be dissected in *The Chronicle of Higher Education* and the subject of such acrimony." Baker did not "think through the unintended consequences"? How is it possible that a professor at a university such as Duke made a decision to sign on to such a disgraceful piece of racist verbiage without thinking it through? That makes two of them, both from the same department. One signed due to peer pressure and the other signed it without thinking. I wonder what their students are "thinking" about that.

"Associate Professor Wahneema Lubiano, who was heavily involved in penning the ad's first draft, [said] that the whole process lasted around 48 hours. . . . The idea that we sat around and plotted, 'In what way can we most egregiously hurt the University?' doesn't seem to be how I remember what happened," Nelson said. It "doesn't *seem* to be how I remember what happened"? Lubiano isn't sure if they plotted to hurt the university? Maybe they were only plotting to hurt the lacrosse players.

Professor Pedro Lasch, associate professor of art, art history and visual studies, "recently condemned people who posted things that implied [the boys'] guilt." That one speaks for itself. He had also signed the original ad as did Professor Joe Harris, associate professor of English. He said, "I think you sign on to what you see as the general intent of such an ad. I did not read the ad as to coming to any judgment in the case." He added, "Would I have written the prose differently? Perhaps." So he wouldn't have necessarily written it that way, but he had no problem signing it with the others. He, like the others, still can't admit the true implications of the ad. How is it possible that these people are still walking through this affair with blinders on in an environment where the majority of people who saw the ad were critical of them for their "rush to judgment" of guilt and their public attack on the lacrosse team?

The article also stated that "The professors do not really understand the outpouring of anger. One cited a conspiracy." Their obvious implication is that the people who spoke out against the Group of 88 were the ones who had the conspiracy, not the Group itself. Diane Nelson added, "Signatories said they never meant to hurt the players. 'The lacrosse players' voices were being heard—our sense was that these other students who have an equal right to be heard were not at that moment." Huh? On what planet does this person reside? The lacrosse players' voices were being heard? When was that? When they were ordered into the police crime lab to have their photos taken and submit to DNA testing? When their team was shut down and their coach was fired? When they were indicted, arrested, and charged with rape, sexual assault, and kidnapping? When they were suspended from school? When the potbangers and the New Black Panthers stormed their house? When the Group of 88 put out their offensive ad? Their statement is so outrageous that it defies belief. The Group was so worried about the students who needed to have "equal rights" "at that very moment" that they drafted their ad to speak up for them . . . at a time when three innocent boys, who, by the way, were also Duke students, were being railroaded and condemned by a whole host of prejudicial, intellectually dishonest bigots. Those Group members who sent out a message of hate, which (according to K.C. Johnson of Durham-in-Wonderland), "was endorsed by three academic departments and thirteen academic programs," are whining now because they were proven wrong and people blasted them for it. In spite of all of the "thousands" of e-mails and numerous articles and blog postings speaking out against their ad, they cannot consider for one moment that their ad just might not have been such a great idea at the time because it was, at the very least, a statement of implied guilt. This is sad because these people just don't seem to get it. Does not one single member of this group have the courage, intellectual integrity, or decency to simply accept some responsibility for their actions and just apologize to the boys for being too quick to judge them? I respectfully submit that perhaps we need to do a better job of evaluating those we are trusting to educate our children.

On January 22, 2007, as quoted in a newsobserver.com article dated February 3, 2007, entitled "Easley: Nifong Broke His Word," North Carolina Governor Mike Easley criticized Nifong for the way he handled the lacrosse case, especially the statements that Nifong made in which he publicly declared that the lacrosse players had committed a racially motivated gang rape. Easley said that "picking Nifong to be Durham's District Attorney was the worst appointment of [my] career." Commenting about Nifong's promise not to run in the district attorney election in 2006, "Easley told law students in New

York that Nifong's decision to seek office in last fall's election almost prompted him to consider yanking Nifong from office." The article quotes Easley as saying that "I almost un-appointed him when he decided to run. . . . I rate that as probably the poorest appointment that I've. . . ." The article said, "[Easley] trailed off before adding 'I've made some good ones.'" Also according to the article, when asked by an audience member how he rated Nifong's handling of the lacrosse case, Easley responded that "Nifong had done a poor job."

On January 24, 2007, the North Carolina Bar amended its complaint to add new charges alleging that Nifong made numerous "extrajudicial statements" to the media that "he knew or reasonably should have known would have a substantial likelihood of materially prejudicing an adjudicative proceeding" and "heightening public condemnation of the accused."

In other words, the damning comments Nifong had made to the press made it highly unlikely that the Duke Three would receive a fair trial. The complaint also addresses the agreement Nifong and Meehan made about keeping the exculpatory material from the defendants; the fact that Nifong never disclosed the exculpatory information to the defendants; that Nifong "repeatedly misrepresented to the Court and the defense counsel that he had provided all potentially exculpatory evidence"; that Nifong denied knowing about the "potentially exculpatory DNA evidence"; and that by misrepresenting that his agreement with Meehan was "based on privacy concerns," "Nifong engaged in conduct prejudicial to the administration of justice." The reference to privacy concerns is in regard to one of Nifong's bogus claims that the reason he didn't want the potentially exculpatory information (the test results showing that the DNA of several non-lacrosse players had been found in Mangum) in Meehan's report was because he wanted to protect the identity of the suspects. That was an insane excuse considering that

Nifong had consistently advertised who the suspects were—forty-six members of the Duke lacrosse team!

The North Carolina State Bar requested "that disciplinary action be taken against Nifong." Many lawyers believe that the D.A. is not only in jeopardy of being disbarred, meaning that he may lose his license to practice law, he may also eventually find himself *behind* bars. In fact, according to a recent *Newsday* article entitled "Duke DA Backlash," there is strong Congressional support for a federal investigation of Nifong.

In essence, the charges against Nifong include his conspiracy with Dr. Meehan to withhold the exculpatory DNA results from the defense (information that could have helped prove their innocence), "misleading commentary" (the inflammatory and misleading statements that Nifong had been making to the media about the Duke lacrosse team members), and "dishonesty, fraud, deceit, or misrepresentation" (in particular, his statements about the possibility that Mangum's alleged attackers used condoms, in spite of the SANE report that had stated otherwise). The Complaint and the Amended Complaint that were filed against Nifong are impressive in that the allegations contained in them are ones that are supported by well-documented, hard evidence. In most cases, a complaint will set forth allegations that the person bringing the claim believes he or she will be able to prove. The validity of the claims will eventually be decided by conflicting testimony from witnesses or by a theory established through circumstantial evidence. In this case, each of the Bar's allegations against Nifong is one that can clearly and easily be proven by recorded statements made by Nifong, transcripts of court proceedings in which Nifong participated, or documents generated by Nifong.

In a seven-page December 28, 2006, letter that Nifong addressed to the Bar, and a forty-eight page Memorandum of Law that his attorneys submitted on February 28, 2007, Nifong's defenses were almost as absurd as his behavior in the case itself. His letter regarding his failure to turn over exculpatory DNA evidence was filled with denials. He had the nerve to call the charges against him "career threatening." He all but accused the Bar of making him into a scapegoat, saying that "'word on the street' in prosecutorial circles has been that the North Carolina State Bar, stung by criticism resulting from past decisions . . . is looking for a prosecutor of which to make an example." If that is what they were looking for, they didn't have to look very far in this case, because Nifong certainly made it easy for them. He is refusing to accept responsibility for his actions and is attempting to blame anyone but himself for his misconduct. He simply doesn't get it. Do we see a pattern here? Nifong's outrageous behavior, not some random witch-hunt, is directly responsible for the Bar's complaint.

Nifong also attempted to excuse his failure to turn over the exculpatory DNA evidence by claiming that he *did* turn it over, or that if he didn't turn it over, it was because he was too caught up in his "hotly contested" political campaign and "facing an unusually contentious challenge from an unprecedented number of challengers" (two to be exact) to pay enough attention to the case, that the case was too much of a burden for his legal assistant to handle alone, and his office staff was too overloaded with work from the case to pay attention to the contents of the documents that they copied for him. Consequently, he contended, they didn't realize that anything was missing. He also argued that he assumed that he did nothing wrong since he was never sanctioned by the court for not turning the documents over to defense counsel.

Strangely, in the same letter, he accused a group of bloggers called "The Friends of Duke," who have shown support for the Duke Three since very early on, of "taking it upon themselves to ensure that this case never reaches trial." Calling them "well-connected," "well-financed," but "not well-intentioned," he suggested that the Bar check out their Web site at www.friendsofdukeuniversity.blogspot.com in order to validate that his suggestions aren't a "paranoid delusion." Is he serious? Even if we were to assume that his allegations are accurate, what does it matter if a group of bloggers were admonishing Nifong's handling of the case? Was he implying that they are the reason that the Bar is bringing charges against him? I think the words "paranoid delusion" should be seriously considered in this instance. The fact that he is even attempting to use that as an excuse to the Bar in response to the charges that he is facing may seem incredible, unless we consider his prior highly questionable behavior that gave rise to the complaint against him in the first place.

Nifong ended his letter by saying that he is "disheartened" to have to defend himself against the charges, adding that he is "someone who has always endeavored to fulfill my oath 'to have the criminal laws fairly and impartially administered.'"

Throughout his letter, he also reiterated his claim that "my personal policy since I began felony prosecution in 1979 has been to provide open-file discovery in all my cases. In other words, I was doing what the law now requires 25 years before I had to" (meaning that he had always freely turned over any relevant materials to defense attorneys even before there was a law requiring it.)

In his attorneys' February 28, 2007, response to the Bar, his defenses were simple.

In regard to his inflammatory statements about the Duke Three to the media, Nifong claimed that

1. Since no specific suspects had yet been named when he made the public statements, he was merely trying to "reassure the community that the case was being actively investigated . . . in

an effort to gain assistance on receiving evidence and
information necessary to further the criminal investigation."

That doesn't really make sense and it begs the issue. It is illegal
and unethical for a prosecutor to make public statements of that type
about any pending case, even if the statements are true, which they
aren't! Furthermore, his statements already had the public thinking
that forty-six suspects, Duke lacrosse team members, had, in fact,
been named.

Another one of Nifong's excuses was that

2. His statements were "consistent with matters of public
   record as outlined in the affidavit attached to the
   Application for Nontestimonial Identification Order."

In other words, his claim is that he was merely repeating those
things that Himan put into the application for the NTO and therefore,
if it was misleading, it was Himan's fault. It was the old familiar "He
did it" defense!

3. As for comments that Nifong made after the indictments
   were served, he claimed that he was "entitled" to make them
   "pursuant to comment [7] to Rule 3.6 of the Rules of
   Professional Conduct," which states that "extrajudicial
   statements that might otherwise raise a question under this
   Rule may be permissible when they are made in response to
   statements made publicly by another party, another party's
   lawyer, or third persons, where a reasonable lawyer would
   believe a public response is required in order to avoid
   prejudice to the lawyer's client."

I'm not sure I fully understand this one. Was he saying that it was acceptable to make inflammatory and prejudicial comments about the Duke Three because he was only responding to what bloggers or members of the media were saying about Mangum? That doesn't appear to be an accurate interpretation of the Rules. Further, his most egregious statements were made before any of the boys were indicted in the case. Thus, none of the defense attorneys had come forward yet to publicly defend the boys. So, what exactly was Nifong responding to in defense of his client when he attacked the lacrosse team members?

4. His response also argued that "Defendant further admits that at the time he made 'said statements' that he did not fully understand the extent of the national media interest in this particular investigation and as such, he did not comprehend the effect said statements may have on any matters related to the case."

What? He didn't know any better? He's been handling felony prosecutions for over a quarter of a century and he's claiming that he didn't know what kind of media frenzy would occur in response to allegations of a gang rape involving three white athletes from an elite school such as Duke and a black stripper? Besides, what difference does it make *how much* media coverage there was? *Any* media coverage of such negative comments by a D.A. would be harmful to the suspects in a criminal case. Perhaps Nifong presented this defense in the event that the Bar didn't accept any of his other poor excuses.

5. Nifong also "denied that his comments heightened public condemnation of any particular individual or was intended to do so . . . or that he intended to prejudice any criminal adjudicative proceeding."

As a lawyer, I recognize that a defendant will usually deny allegations in a complaint, but this is a response to a complaint filed by the State Bar against a lawyer. It would not seem advisable for a lawyer/defendant in this situation to deny what appears to clearly be the obvious. Nifong's denial here doesn't really wash when recalling some of his statements, such as "I am satisfied that a sexual assault took place at this residence," or "I would like to think that somebody [not involved in the attack] has the human decency to call up and say, 'What am I doing covering up for a bunch of hooligans?'"

In regard to Nifong's "Dishonesty, Fraud, Deceit, or Misrepresentation," this charge is aimed directly at Nifong's condom comment, which he attempted to explain away by saying that in his experience, he "has learned that a complaining witness rarely ever knows whether a condom was used in a sexual assault." There are several problems with that argument. It is difficult to believe that a person who is allegedly being raped by three men would not notice if they used condoms, especially someone with Mangum's extensive sexual experience. Wouldn't each of them have to take the time at some point to put one on? Or how about the fact that Mangum alleged that one of them forced her to perform oral sex on him? Wouldn't she know if he was wearing a condom? Mangum also specifically stated that a condom had not been used. That statement in the report does not appear to have been made by a person who was merely guessing.

In response to the allegations in the complaint regarding Nifong's agreement with Dr. Meehan to withhold the exculpatory DNA results, he presented the following:

1. Since no trial date had been set, Nifong was not under any obligation to turn them over.

In other words, the State Bar has no grounds to claim that the Duke Three's due process rights and constitutional rights to a fair trial had been violated, since there was no trial date set. The problem here is that the statute that requires Nifong to turn over exculpatory evidence does not make it conditional upon a trial date being set. Further, how can you have a fair trial when you don't have all of the information you need to defend yourself? So much for open discovery laws.

Nifong claimed that at the time of his meeting with Meehan, the one where they conspired to hold back the relevant part of the results, "his attention was not focused on whether trace DNA from individuals not members of the Duke lacrosse team which was found on certain items tested . . . would affect the outcome of any subsequent trial."

Is he arguing that if he didn't focus on it, it shouldn't count? Could this mean that he is admitting that he was intentionally ignoring any exculpatory evidence? The fact that he was not even paying attention to exculpatory evidence would seem to indicate that he was only interested in bringing these charges against these particular defendants and attempting to convict them rather than seeking justice for all parties as he is required by law to do.

2. He also denied that he agreed to have the summary report include only positive results in an effort to prevent the Duke defendants from knowing there was evidence that could prove their innocence, because, he argued, the data submitted with it contained that information.

However, in order to get that information from the data, you would require substantial resources, a team of attorneys, a fine-tooth comb, and a prosecutor who was forthcoming with information.

3. Incredibly, he also claimed, in contradiction to Gottlieb, Himan, and Meehan, that he had no recollection of the

meeting with Meehan on April 10, 2006, the day that the others stated the meeting took place where they were informed that none of the DNA matched Finnerty and Seligmann.

4. Nifong admitted that A.D.A. David Saacks included in the application for the NTO that "DNA evidence requested will immediately rule out any innocent persons," but Nifong claimed that he wasn't responsible for the promises made by the people who work for him.

In summary, it appears that Nifong believes that he can avoid any disciplinary action from the Bar and wiggle his way out of the mess that he's created by offering numerous excuses that place the blame on other people or things: that he was too busy; that his employees were incompetent; that Saacks made a promise that Nifong wasn't obligated to keep; that the police lied to him; that he thought he was complying with the law when he wasn't; that he had to wait to be sanctioned to know whether or not he was complying with the law; that he wasn't focusing on even the possibility that the boys might be innocent; that he was too busy to know what was going on around him; that his condemning statements were only things he said in defense of his client; and on and on ad nauseam. Who is in charge of that office? Whatever happened to "the buck stops here"? How can the lead prosecutor in a case, the District Attorney himself, a man with over twenty-five years of experience, say that he wasn't ultimately responsible for what transpired in his office?

But it didn't end there. Nifong's barrage of excuses continued with his attorneys' March 16, 2007, filing of a brief in support of their motion to dismiss the case. The brief reiterates much of what was said before, and adds that under the U.S. Supreme Court case of

Brady v. Maryland, which states that the "Suppression by the prosecution of evidence favorable to an accused who has requested it violates due process where the evidence is material either to guilt or to punishment, irrespective of the good faith or bad faith of the prosecution." In other words, the fact that Nifong failed to turn over the potentially exculpatory DNA results to the defendants' attorneys is a violation of the Duke Three's rights, whether or not Nifong did it on purpose. Again, the argument that Nifong's brief makes is that the only way the defendants' due process rights would have been violated was if the defendants were denied the right to a fair trial. Since no trial had occurred as of yet, Nifong's attorneys argued that there was no violation.

Further, in regard to Nifong's failure to comply with discovery rules and the court's order to turn over the requested materials to the defense, the brief states that, under the North Carolina General Statutes Section 15A-903, Nifong was only required to turn over the materials "within a reasonable time prior to trial" and that he did, in fact, turn them over. Again, they were pointing to the fact that there had been no trial, thus no violation. However, they failed to see the significance in the Bar's allegations that Nifong had consistently misrepresented to the court and defense counsel that he had turned over the potentially exculpatory materials and that he also represented to the court that he was not even aware of those materials, "or, alternatively, was not aware of their exclusion from DSI's report." Further, there is little doubt that the agreement made between Nifong and Meehan regarding the omission in the report of potentially exculpatory material is what weighs much heavier on Nifong than whether or not Nifong finally did reveal the truth, albeit with arm twisting and having his neck slipped into a noose.

Apparently, Nifong still doesn't get it.

After all of the attempts that the defense and the court made to obtain the missing discovery materials from Nifong, it has become more than clear that had nobody learned that part of the DNA report was missing, Nifong would have continued holding it back, the court would have never ordered him to turn the materials over, and he would not have come under scrutiny by the Bar. In other words, he is now putting the cart before the horse in claiming that he did comply, and it doesn't matter when or why he eventually complied, because in his seemingly distorted sense of reality, he thinks he can convince those involved that his act of finally complying is *all* that should matter today. Following that line of reasoning, I have to wonder if there are other times when Nifong has gotten away with this type of behavior.

The most egregious claim that the brief makes is in regard to Nifong's failure to turn over "memorializations of Dr. Meehan's oral statements" regarding the DNA test results. In other words, Nifong had conversations with Dr. Meehan that were relevant to the case and he never took notes of those discussions and turned them over to the defense. The brief states two arguments in regard to that issue. The first involves semantics. Incredibly, Nifong is asserting that the statute in question "failed to specifically define what the term 'statement' encompassed." Thus, the brief argues, it was not clear to Nifong that he was obligated to write down what Meehan had said during their "forgettable" meeting on April 10, 2006.

The second part of the argument is that those memorializations were attorney "work product," and therefore, according to Nifong's attorneys, they are protected from disclosure under the state's criminal discovery statutes. To explain that more clearly, there are certain issues that an attorney may discuss in preparation of a case that fall under the definition of "attorney work product," which are materials prepared by an attorney in anticipation of or during the course of litigation. The reason for the protection is that certain materials may relate to an attorney's strategy as to how he will handle the litigation and revealing that information would put the opposing counsel at a distinct advantage. However, a discussion between a prosecutor and an expert witness where an arrangement is made to exclude certain test results from a report intended for use in a criminal case is not considered attorney work product, especially when the agreement involves withholding information crucial to a defendant's defense and where a defendant is legally entitled to full disclosure of all of those test results.

Under Nifong's premise, it would be up to a prosecutor's discretion to obtain all test results verbally and pick and choose which ones would go into a written report without fear that any exculpatory information would ever be revealed to a defense attorney—which is exactly what Nifong appears to have attempted to do here!

There is one more issue that the brief raises in defense of Nifong. In regard to Nifong's failure "to provide the Duke Defendants with the results of the NTO identification process," the claim is that "the statute does not set out any specific format in which the 'report' must be; only that the information must be provided." Thus, since Nifong eventually handed it over, he didn't violate the statute.

On March 19, 2007, the North Carolina State Bar filed a Memorandum of Law in Opposition to [Nifong's] Motion to Dismiss stating that "Nifong now seeks to have a claim that he violated the Rules of Professional Conduct dismissed on the grounds that his successful deception of the Court resulted in a Court order which did not specifically require him to provide memorializations of Dr. Meehan's statements." To put it plainly, due to Nifong's consistent claim that he had turned everything over to the defense and that the DNA report contained everything that was discussed between him and Dr. Meehan, Nifong had convinced the court not to order him to have Dr. Meehan put down on paper what he and Meehan had discussed and turn it over to them. Therefore, he reasoned, he was not in violation of the court by not turning it over to them. Incredible!

In arguing against Nifong's request to have his case dismissed, the Memorandum states that Nifong would like the Bar Association to believe that it was not a violation of the Rules for him to "discuss and be keenly aware of potentially exculpatory DNA test results [with Dr. Meehan] and direct or agree that those results would not be contained in a report provided to indicted defendants and other named suspects," and "successfully and repeatedly deceive courts into entering orders finding falsely that he had had no previous discussions about these potentially exculpatory DNA test results." Nifong thinks his claim should be dismissed because he believes that "he had absolute discretion to withhold potentially exculpatory information of which he was fully aware until some unspecified time prior to trial without violating the Rules. . . ." Nifong's behavior "implies that he was also entitled to withhold and never disclose any potentially exculpatory information in any case that is settled prior to trial." Under that assumption, Nifong could force the hand of every suspect by making them take a plea bargain for a crime they didn't commit simply because they are convinced that there is no evidence in existence to prove their innocence.

Now that the Bar has brought charges against Nifong and he has formally presented his defenses, we may think we know about all of his wrongful actions in his handling of this case, especially since he has revealed how he is attempting to defend those actions. However, we may not even be aware of some of the worst of it yet, because some of it took place ex parte and behind closed doors, such as the process of obtaining the grand jury indictments. But it's not that difficult to surmise from the following information what probably happened there.

On February 6, 2007, ABC's *Good Morning America* revealed an exclusive look at the people whose job it was to indict Evans,

Finnerty, and Seligmann on charges of rape, sexual offense, and kidnapping. In an article entitled "Exclusive: Duke Lacrosse Jurors Speak Out," which detailed the *Good Morning America* segment, two members of the grand jury anonymously expressed why they recently had a change of heart. Unable to discuss what actually took place in the grand jury room due to legal constraints, one juror commented that "Knowing what I know now . . . I think I would have definitely made a different decision." Continuing, he added, "I don't think I could have made a decision to go forward with the charges that were put before us. I don't think those charges would have been the proper charges, based on what I know now." The other juror commented, "I don't know for sure whether she was raped, you know, because of everything that . . . came out. I'm not sure, to tell you the truth."

People need to know why there are no specifics. While laws prohibit them from revealing what went on in the grand jury room, their comments made it clear that they weren't given enough information to make an informed decision. The grand jury process is different than serving on a trial jury in that grand jurors only hear one side of the case—the prosecution's. However, in light of all of the questionable actions that have transpired in this case, I wonder if these grand jurors were presented with creatively misleading information. Certainly, they did not have all of the facts. I suspect that what was presented to grand jurors was as slanted and misleading as what was stated in Himan's affidavit in support of the application for the NTO. The article offered some information that I did not find surprising: the only witnesses to testify and present evidence to the grand jury were Gottlieb and Himan.

When interviewers on *Good Morning America* asked for the grand jurors' reaction to Nifong dropping the rape charges, the second grand juror exclaimed, "What do you mean you're not sure whether you got raped or not?" The first juror said that it raised a lot of questions. "If you're dropping the rape charges, why are you even going to try to go forward with charges of assault and kidnapping? If no rape occurred, why, why go ahead and try to . . . prosecute on other charges?"

The first juror summed up the whole incident: "A lot of people will be affected by this. If they are found not guilty, and we do [find] out that no assault or kidnapping happened . . . then you have a lot of lives that were directly affected. You can't go back and undo any of this."

I can only think of David Evans's mother's words when *60 Minutes* correspondent Lesley Stahl asked Rae Evans what she would say to Nifong if he were in the room, "Mr. Nifong, you've picked on the wrong family . . . and you will pay every day for the rest of your life." Her words are coming to pass.

11

THE EDUCATION OF ATHLETICS

As the case neared its resolution, Nifong wasn't the only one who was being forced to answer for his misconduct in the lacrosse fiasco. There was a growing undercurrent in the campus community calling for Brodhead to resign. In fact, that sentiment is especially spreading throughout Duke alumni circles. A huge number of Duke grads are incensed about the way that Brodhead and the school's administrators treated the boys during the months that followed Mangum's allegations.

In April of 2006, shortly after Mangum brought her allegations, I traveled to Durham for a reunion with some of my former teammates. My good friend Leo Hart, who was our quarterback, arranged for a large number of the guys to get together for a dinner at the Washington Duke Inn. It was great fun, just a bunch of former Duke football players who played together over a period of about four or five years, getting together for a night of catching up, reminiscing, and enjoying each other's company again. The group included my former roommate, Phil Asack, along with Wes Chesson, Bob Shinn, Dick Biddle, Bob Fitch, and many others. This group of former athletes, which represents a typical example of what Duke produces, included several guys who played professionally in the NFL, as well as doctors, lawyers, engineers, corporate executives, highly successful businessmen, and other accomplished professionals. During the dinner, we were having a good time, telling war stories and passing the microphone around. Everybody got up and told on each other. You can imagine the scene: people laughing and having fun all around. With former teammates, it is like visiting with family. Even if you haven't seen each other for years, you pick up right where you left off. But in the midst of all of that fun, levity, and reminiscing of good times past, a surprising thing happened. A few people, when they took the microphone, spoke about the lacrosse case. There were strong, emotional statements about what a travesty the whole fiasco was, and how disappointed people were with how the Duke administration was handling the case. Specifically, they were denouncing the administration and calling for Brodhead to be ousted as president of the university due to the way he was treating the lacrosse players and his firing of Coach Pressler. Obviously, the situation weighed heavily on many people's minds, or they would not have brought up the somber subject so passionately in the midst of such fun and levity.

Another old friend, Dan Smith, who was one of my fraternity brothers at Duke, was so outraged by Brodhead's treatment of the boys that he sent the following letter to him:

President Richard H. Brodhead:

I write you at this time as a concerned alum in reference to the affect your leadership or rather the lack thereof is having on Duke University. I have watched from afar since last spring as this tragedy has unfolded in the National and World press. I must tell you President Brodhead the actions that you have taken and equally as important, the actions you have chosen not to take can only be described as disgusting.

So you better understand my point of departure on your performance, let me advise you of what I have done professionally since leaving Duke. I have prosecuted criminal cases on the local level (Denver Colorado District Attorneys Office) Organized Crime cases on the State level (Special assistant

Attorney General for Colorado) and all types of Federal crime as an Assistant United States Attorney for the District of Colorado. For the past twenty-five years I have actively defended individuals and companies who have been charged with federal or state crimes all over the United States.

From the earliest reports of the so-called Lacrosse scandal it was clear that the investigation and later case wreaked [sic] of an ill planned financial grab by the so-called victim and the worst sort of political opportunism by Mr. Nifong. I understand from press reports, including interviews which you have given, that you had the information which showed this case for what it was early in its infancy. Your own police department told you the so-called victim was lying. The evidence which then kept coming into the public domain clearly established the allegations here to be nothing but bogus.

For some reason you forcefully chose to take the side of what we now know to be two pathological liars. Why? Certainly the judgment exercised by members of the [lacrosse] team was ill advised, but you chose to: suspend the season, effectively fire the coach, and suspend two young men and students who had only been *charged* with criminal conduct. I was and still am unaware as to when the Bill of Rights was suspended at Duke University.

Obviously with the personnel you have at Duke you must have received competent legal advice. You have a professor at your law school who has written and spoken widely on Mr. Nifong's lack of ethical conduct since the inception of the investigation. I read with great interest a summary of a talk you gave at the recent football summit at Duke. You are quoted as saying "I embrace athletics at Duke" (*Blue Devil Weekly*, January 20, 2007). My God, President Brodhead, if the way you treated those three players, the team, and the coach is your idea of an embrace, what do you do when you dislike someone or something?

I suppose my last straw was watching the families of these three players interviewed on CBS TV. When one mother said she would never let her son return to Duke it broke my heart. But what should we expect [after] the way her son has been treated. I am sure [Finnerty and Seligmann] matriculated at Duke expecting to earn their degrees, obtain a valuable education, and enjoy their time in college. A Duke degree is something to cherish for many reasons, but you for unjustifiable reasons have denied them their dream.

I can only surmise that your knee jerk reaction to the events as they unfolded was kindled by the naive, ignorant and well-publicized response of a significant number of the Duke faculty. Your decision to quickly place the blame on a "White Duke" and then your jumping onto Jesse [Jackson's] race wagon is appalling. On an almost monthly basis I read the Duke magazine and the online newsletter. Each always contains articles of efforts by Duke students to leave the Durham community a better place than they found it. In that regard not a lot has changed at Duke from the 1960s. My living group and I participated annually throughout the year in providing tutoring and coaching to elementary school children who attended a school we had adopted.

President Brodhead, I well remember standing on the main quadrangle next to then President Sanford and admiring his leadership abilities in quelling an ugly disturbance that had broken out on campus. His leadership brought Duke through some difficult times. I would recommend that you study and learn from his efforts. If that isn't possible President Brodhead then please return at your earliest convenience to the ivy covered walls in New Haven.

DANIEL T. SMITH

(Trinity College 1970)

What Dan stated in this letter reflects some of the sentiments of many alumni and friends of Duke on this subject. And I suspect that Dan's was only one of many letters sent to Brodhead that were critical of the manner in which he was handling the situation. People are very upset because Brodhead has done irreparable harm to our alma mater. For a man who was apparently concerned about public relations more than anything else, including the welfare of his students, he has tarnished Duke's image before the entire nation. This was either done out of sheer incompetence, or he was driven by an agenda that is certainly not in the best interest of the school.

While Brodhead took the ball and ran with it in the wrong direction, it is clear who is responsible for pushing this case to the extreme. Of course, it began late one night with Mangum's false allegations of what had happened to her, but do we really believe that what she had to say was so convincing that it caused Nifong to risk everything he had worked for to prosecute a false claim of rape? I don't believe that. Clearly, Nifong wanted to win the election. Mangum apparently didn't want to go to the drunk tank. Gottlieb apparently wanted to appease the neighbors and his own hostility toward the Duke students. The Group of 88 wanted to further their social agendas, and so on. Others, like the New Black Panthers, knew what would likely result from their actions, and they continued with their hate crusades anyway.

Mangum may be too disturbed to fully understand the magnitude and consequences of her false allegations. As mentioned earlier, Mangum may have documented psychiatric problems, and she may have felt that once she made her accusations, she couldn't admit that she had only lied in order to stay out of Durham Access. I would have hoped that by now, more than one year after her allegations had been made, Mangum would have come forward with the truth. There were rumors that she was not cooperating with the new prosecutors from the North Carolina Attorney General's Office, Jim Coman and Mary Winstead, but the Attorney General's Office issued a denial. After I had learned about the evidence that weighed so heavily in favor of the boys, it became obvious to me that the only thing Mangum had left was her own testimony, as there was nothing else, actual or contrived, which could possibly support her claim of sexual assault and kidnapping. It would seem that all of those individuals who were so hell-bent on benefiting from Mangum's false allegations didn't really take into consideration what they were getting themselves into.

Unfortunately, one person did derive *some* benefit from this travesty, as short-lived as it now appears to be. Mangum's lie gave Nifong the platform that he needed to gain support for his campaign, and the boys were just in the wrong place at the right time for him. Mangum's agenda had nothing to do with Nifong. Nifong's agenda, however, and his continuation with a case that had no basis, in fact, is a different story. He knew better. He knew the truth. To borrow some of Ruth Sheehan's words:

Mr. Nifong, you knew.

We know you knew.

I do not purport to know all there is to know about this case, but I have learned a great deal about it. While no one can ever be absolutely certain how any legal case will end up, an honest and competent prosecutor in good faith would have dismissed this case based upon the facts that had been revealed. Even if we were to ignore all of evidence that clearly weighs in favor of the boys' innocence, and a prosecutor felt compelled to proceed with the charges, he or she would have to totally rely upon the testimony and credibility of the two dancers. Assuming that Mangum and Roberts were willing to testify and expose themselves to the likelihood of brutal cross-examination, if not to potential prosecution for perjury or making false statements to law enforcement officers, they would have zero credibility based on their conflicting and inconsistent statements, not to mention their criminal actions in the past. They each have made numerous statements that are totally inconsistent with the overwhelming weight of the evidence. They each made numerous statements that are inconsistent with their own prior statements, and they each made statements that are inconsistent with each other's statements.

Clearly, no prosecution could have any reasonable chance of success if it had to be carried by the testimony or credibility of either or both of the dancers. In fact, the North Carolina Attorney General Roy Cooper obviously concurs. On April 11, 2007, at a press conference that brought with it as much fanfare as when Nifong first made his incriminating comments about the lacrosse players, Cooper made the long-awaited announcement that after a thorough investigation, all charges against Evans, Finnerty, and Seligmann were being dropped. In his announcement, Cooper cited, as mentioned throughout this book, the numerous contradictions in Mangum's versions of what had allegedly occurred, the photographic and phone record evidence, the "faulty and unreliable" eyewitness photo identification procedures, the lack of any DNA evidence that points to any of the accused, and the fact that there are no corroborating witnesses to support the accusations. However, Cooper went even further. In an almost unprecedented move for a prosecutor at this juncture in a case, he didn't just say that there wasn't enough evidence to support the charges or that the boys are not guilty of the charges; he came out and declared that the three boys are *innocent*.

Calling the cases against the Duke Three "a tragic rush to accuse and a failure to verify serious allegations," Cooper condemned Nifong's handling of the case by saying that "with the weight of the state behind him, the Durham District attorney pushed forward unchecked." He further stated that "there were many points in this case where caution would have served justice better than bravado." Continuing, he added that "in the rush to condemn a community and a state, [Nifong] lost the ability to see clearly. Regardless of the reasons that this case was pushed forward, the result was wrong. Today we need to learn from this and keep it from happening again to anybody!"

Cooper also stated that "this case shows the enormous consequences of overreaching by a prosecutor," and he stressed that "what has been learned here is that the internal checks on a criminal charge, sworn statements, reasonable grounds, proper suspect photo lineups, accurate and fair discovery, all are critically important." He then proposed a law that would give the North Carolina Supreme Court the "authority to remove a case from a prosecutor in limited circumstances."

As a lawyer, Duke alumnus, and a father of college-age children, I applaud Roy Cooper for having the courage, professional integrity, and human decency to make these powerful statements. He not only displayed a great deal of professional responsibility by taking this stand, but he demonstrated how effective the truth can be when used fairly to allow the criminal justice system to finally work properly.

On April 12, 2007, the day after Cooper declared Evans, Finnerty, and Seligmann innocent of all charges, Nifong issued a long-overdue and hollow apology: "To the extent that I made judgments that ultimately proved to be incorrect, I apologize to the three students that were wrongly accused." Considering all that Nifong had done to pursue the criminal charges against the Duke Three, it isn't surprising that his statement was not taken seriously by those who had been involved in the case. In the words of Reade Seligmann's attorney, Jim Cooney, "You can accept an apology from someone who knows all the facts and simply makes an error," but "if a person refuses to know all the facts and then makes a judgment, that's far worse, particularly when that judgment destroys lives."

To date, neither Richard Brodhead nor Robert Steel has issued an apology to these young men or their families. In fact, early on April 12, 2007, Steel made the following comment in an e-mail he sent to the Duke community: "As we look back and with the benefit of what we now know there is no question that there are some things that might have been done differently. However, anyone critical of President Brodhead should be similarly critical of the entire board." That is good advice for those who wish to see real changes made at Duke University!

This brutal nightmare has now finally come to a long overdue conclusion for Evans, Finnerty, Seligmann, and their families. But this travesty of justice has left its mark. There are many victims in this case, though none as tragically scarred as Evans, Finnerty, and Seligmann, and their families. I will never forget the cover of a national magazine that came out shortly after the accusations were made against the lacrosse team. It displayed a picture of Duke lacrosse players with big, bold letters that read: "Sex, Lies, & Duke."

Duke University was caught in the crossfire as well, and the wounds suffered there will take some time to heal. The athletic department bore the brunt of it, from the firing of Coach Pressler to the devastating suspension of the lacrosse team, preventing them from making a legitimate run at a national championship. This incredible travesty also tarnished the school's reputation and placed a dark cloud over Duke athletics. And the athletic programs at Duke are a big part of what makes Duke such a special place. When combined with the level of education offered there, having highly successful athletic teams competing at the highest collegiate level only serves to enhance the school's overall environment. However, there are apparently some people who don't like the fact that the two are intertwined at Duke and college campuses in general. The lacrosse case exposed the fact that some professors and administrators at Duke feel that athletics are unnecessary and only serve to interfere with the academic environment.

While on the Duke campus, I spoke to Law School Professor Paul Haagan about that. Haagan had experience as special university counsel to the National Collegiate Athletic Association (NCAA) and for twenty years he has been advising athletes who have been entering the field of professional sports. He was also the head of Duke's Academic Council and initiated a program in 2006 to assign faculty members to sports teams.

After Mangum's allegations were brought, approximately fifty professors joined together in June 2006 to ask Brodhead for more faculty oversight and a closer examination of athletics. Haagan came up with a plan to give faculty members a closer look at what the life of a Duke athlete is really like. However, Haagan's recent replacement, the newly elected chairperson of Duke's Academic Council and Group of 88 member Paula McClain disagreed with Haagan at the time that he suggested his plan.

In a September 21, 2006, Newsobserver.com article entitled "Duke Sports Idea Roils Professors," McClain commented that "people are aghast that it's being considered." Apparently, she had been communicating with an anti-athletic group of professors roaming the Duke campus who have a latent hostility toward college athletic programs. Some of these people are quick to suggest that sports programs should be shut down. One of them actually took the position that lacrosse had to be shut down for four years until this particular group of players was flushed out of the system. Another created a parody of Haagan's plan called "Coaches Academic Associates Program," which invites coaches to "participate in the academic environment to better understand what Duke students experience."

One of the most unsettling occurrences related to campus athletics last year was the appointment of Professor Peter Wood as chair of the Campus Cultural Initiative Committee's subgroup on athletics. Wood has been outspoken about his impression of Duke athletes, apparently from high up on his pedestal. I came across a September 11, 2006, article entitled "Peter Wood's Distorted Campus Culture," on the Durham-in-Wonderland blog that quotes a comment Peter Wood made to the *New York Times* on April 1, 2006, a mere two weeks after Mangum's allegations rocked the Duke campus. The blog article stated that "Wood offered [the *New York Times*] an interpretation of athletics at Duke dripping with the condescension of a figure safely ensconced in the upper middle class." Wood was quoted saying, "The football players here . . . are often rural white boys with baseball caps or hard-working black students who are proud to be at Duke." Wood's propensity to inappropriately label stereotypes is only exceeded by his arrogance and totally inaccurate view of the students who attend the school at which he purports to teach.

And who can forget Karla Holloway's proud denunciation of men's sports during the summer of 2006 when she wrote her scathing article entitled "The Cultural Value of Sport: Title IX and Beyond"(discussed in chapter 5). She didn't mince words when she commented about the "lacrosse team's notion of who was in service of whom and the presumption of privilege that their elite sports' performance had earned. . . ." She went further though, talking about Duke, "where the 'culture' of sports seems for some a reasonable displacement for the cultures of moral conduct, ethical citizenship and personal integrity." She also commented that "sports reinforces exactly those behaviours of entitlement which have been and can be so abusive to women and girls and those 'othered' by their sports' history of membership."

A stark contrast to Holloway's comments are seen in a June 21, 2006, article on www.newsobserver.com entitled "Coach K Speaks Up for Sports," which discussed a news conference where Coach K "took the opportunity to say [that] critics of Duke athletics are wrong." He stated, "It seemed like this was a good time to attack athletics, not just at Duke but anywhere," adding that "I think the people who do that are very narrow-minded." In response to Coach K, "Orin Starn, professor of cultural anthropology and a self-proclaimed sports fan," was quoted as saying that "there is a growing feeling that athletics occupies an oversized place at Duke. Whether Coach Krzyzewski likes it or not, these are serious issues and issues being raised at colleges around the country."

Coach K argued, "Athletics are an intrinsic part of education at Duke, where 10 percent of students are on teams." He further stated, "Coaches instill lessons in teamwork and loyalty and teach students how to handle success and failure."

Haagan's new program is meant to expand on Coach K's belief that "intercollegiate athletics is . . . an integral part of any university." Haagan has commented that the program he had recommended "would be an informal first step toward fostering more meaningful interaction between the athletic and academic sides of campus."

According to a September 22, 2006, report entitled "Haagan Explains Faculty Athletics Associates Program" on Duke's "News and Communications" page, Haagan said that "Duke invests substantial resources in intercollegiate athletics," but most faculty members have no idea "what happens on those teams. . . . The coaches speak of themselves as teachers and educators, but the form of teaching and education is quite different from the teaching and education on the rest of the campus." Haagan also said, "The proposal would give faculty members unprecedented access to athletic teams, including meetings, practice sessions, and occasional trips to away games." On Thursday, September 21, 2006, during an Academic Council meeting, Haagan announced that the Academic Council's Executive Committee had approved his new plan, the "Faculty Athletics Associates Program." According to Haagan, eighty faculty members were already anxious to participate in the program.

There is no way around the fact that athletics are an important part of university life. There is a strong sense of toughness, commitment, loyalty, and work ethic instilled in college athletes that can only serve them well, both in and beyond their academic lives. Working as part of a team helps young people recognize the need to share in the responsibilities that go along with operating in unison and watching out for teammates. They recognize that when their team wins, it is due to the efforts of all players working together as a team, rather than one person trying to be a star. And when their team loses, players must share in the responsibility of their defeat rather than point the finger at others. It doesn't take a rocket scientist to understand that when an athlete participates in a sport that he or she truly enjoys, it gives him or her a sense of accomplishment and a feeling of well-being. The drive to compete, the discipline to do what it takes to succeed, the confidence an athlete gains from success, and the character-growing process of having to sometimes deal with failure are among the things that are learned through participation in sports that are invaluable tools for any student. It is no coincidence that I and many of my teammates earned better grades during football season than we did when we had a less disciplined schedule during the off season.

In reflecting back on all of the verbal attacks that were flung at the lacrosse team, the Duke Three, and athletes in general, I feel it is necessary to say something about the type of athletic, intellectual, and moral character that is expected of the students at Duke University who participate in the school's athletic programs. Duke does not recruit an athlete unless that person is well qualified academically. The athletes at Duke live among the student body and have the same academic work loads and take the same courses as all other well-qualified students at the school. The main difference between the experience that an athlete has from that of a nonathlete at Duke is the many hours each day that the athlete must spend training, practicing, attending meetings, and participating in other time and energy consuming activities related to their sport. The academic standards established at Duke for its athletes to remain eligible to participate in their sports programs is higher than what is required by the Atlantic Coast Conference (ACC) and the National Collegiate Athletic Association (NCAA). The graduation rate for athletes at Duke is also higher than the graduation rate for nonathletes within the student body.

Due to the obvious risk that those reading what I have written will view my opinion as the biased sentiments of a die-hard former Duke athlete, I am going to refer you to a February 12, 2007 article that quotes a new NCAA study that focuses on the value of college athletics. The findings show that athletic programs are a true benefit to students. The following are some of the statistics pointed out in the article posted on the NCAA Web site (www.ncaa.org) entitled "Research Validates Value, and Values, of Athletics."

- Eighty-eight percent of student-athletes earn their degrees.

- Eighty-three percent of student-athletes have positive feelings about their choice of major.

- Ninety-one percent of former Division I student-athletes have full-time jobs, and on average, their income levels are higher than non-student-athletes.

- Twenty-seven percent of former Division I student-athletes go on to earn a postgraduate degree.

The article calls the study, which involved two different surveys and a combined total of twenty-eight thousand athletes, including eight thousand former student-athletes who entered college in 1994 and twenty thousand current student-athletes, "perhaps the most ambitious and comprehensive" study ever performed on student-athlete experiences. It also summarized the above statistics by stating that "student-athletes are at least as engaged academically as their student-body counterparts, they graduate at higher rates, and they believe their athletics participation benefited their careers."

These impressive statistics speak for themselves. As a former Duke athlete, I can certainly vouch for how I benefited from participating in college football, as did many other former college athletes that I have known over the years. But the study puts the situation into the proper perspective, one that validates the fact that the benefits of participating in athletics does much more for athletes than enhance their physical capabilities, bring them a little fame, and award them a trophy. This study should help put to rest the notion that athletics is not an essential part of the college curriculum and also that members of the Duke Men's Lacrosse Team were a bunch of "hooligans."

On February 24, 2007, the Duke Blue Devils men's lacrosse team made their triumphant return to the field at Koskinen Stadium in their first official game since their sudden suspension in March 2006 amid the allegations of rape by Mangum. In front of a cheering near-record crowd of 6,485 fans, the team emerged from an inflatable tunnel and ran onto the field through a cloud of pyrotechnic smoke to take victory over Dartmouth by a score of 17–11. It was time. The smoke was for effect, but to those whose emotions were running high, it was symbolic of an almost shattered team rising up from the dark cloud that besieged them not too long ago. More than sixty media crews were there, another record for a lacrosse game. Nobody knew what to expect considering what the players had been forced to endure over the past year.

Prior to the game, players were seen wearing black warm-up jerseys bearing the numbers 6, 13, and 45, the jersey numbers of Evans, Finnerty, and Seligmann, their teammates who at the time of the game, still faced charges of sexual assault and kidnapping. Fans crowded the stands wearing buttons with slogans such as "Fantastic Lies" and "Innocent Until Proven Innocent."

Students were prohibited from carrying signs into the stadium, but the university posted some on the fence lining the field. They contained the Latin phrase *succisa virescit*, which is the motto for The Delbarton School in Morristown, New Jersey, where Reade Seligmann and three current Blue Devils had attended high school. The Duke lacrosse program began using it in preseason. Its meaning is extremely fitting: "When cut down, it grows back stronger."

There were only supporters at this lacrosse event, a pleasant departure from what the team endured only a short time ago. Spirits ran high, and for a brief moment, everything was right with the world for the members of the Duke lacrosse team. After their win, they left the field to the sounds of cheering fans.

Through the tragedy that took its toll on last year's lacrosse team, it is obvious that they not only became stronger, they matured to a level well beyond their years. They have endured an experience that is very rare for anyone, let alone young college students. In attempting to put a positive light on what has been a very dark year for the lacrosse players, the team's new head coach, John Danowski, was quoted in Duke's newspaper, *The Chronicle* in a March 8, 2007, article entitled "The Things They Learned" saying, "This whole experience is going to be a blessing as all these kids get older. It's going to be an unbelievable experience, just a hell of a thing to live through."

Danowski has a challenging job right now, coaching the team that he says is "still [finding it] difficult to think and talk about last spring." He described the "emotions associated with being on trial in front of the public, with being branded 'hooligans' and 'rapists' and with watching three close friends face long jail sentences. . . . These young men have been accused of racism and sexism and they have seen three of their friends charged with much worse. And they were forced to stand by while those three friends had their faces splashed on the cover of magazines and newspapers all over the country with headlines calling them rapists."

As seen throughout the chapters of this book, there are individuals who feel comfortable pigeonholing others into stereotypes, defining them by assigned labels, categories existing only in their morally objectionable thought patterns. They look at kids such as those on the Duke lacrosse team and immediately classify them as spoiled, elitist, rich jocks who are sexist and racist and think they can get away with anything.

But, the problem does not lie with the lacrosse team, boys who were simply doing what good kids do to make the best of their futures. In truth, the problem lies with those individuals who find the need to point out the perceived deficiencies of others. As demonstrated in this book, there were many people who were willing to prejudge the lacrosse players and throw them to the wolves without so much as seeing the evidence that would prove their innocence.

We have seen it firsthand—the hate and bigotry that brought an entire town, a great university, its lacrosse team, and the lives of three innocent young men and their families to a grinding halt. But they will all rise again, stronger as a result of this experience. The ascension has already begun, from the team's emersion back onto the lacrosse field and the top of the national rankings to the eloquent words of one of their captains, Ed Douglas, who stated, "One of the things we've learned is how myopic stereotypes are, either of the lacrosse team, or of the student group or of the community itself." He continued, "Durham has been portrayed in a particularly negative light. I think we recognize there have been failures in the characterization of people and of places throughout this story, but that's a lesson we've learned and hopefully that means that when we interact with people we can break down those stereotypes." That's a pretty incredible piece of hard-earned insight for someone his age, but insight is what we gain through the tough lessons we learn.

Hopefully, nothing like this will never happen again, but if it does, maybe someone will step up and remind those whose knee-jerk reaction is to judge too quickly and jump on the bandwagon of hate about what happened in March of 2006 in Durham, North Carolina, and stop them in their tracks.

On March 13, 2007, exactly one year to the day from the lacrosse party that brought so much distress to so many people, Coach K appeared on an HBO program called *Costas Now,* hosted by broadcaster Bob Costas. The show mainly focused on college athletes, but there was one segment devoted to Coach K. During the interview, Costas asked him some pointed questions about the Duke lacrosse case and how the university handled it. Besides being Duke's head basketball coach, Coach K has the title of Special Assistant to University President Richard Brodhead. When Costas asked him why he did not speak out publicly last spring about the situation when there was so much publicity surrounding it, he stated that when the allegations were made against the boys, he went to Brodhead and told him, "If you need me, you tell me and put me in the position where I'm not the basketball coach, but I am that special assistant to you." Coach K said that "Dick Brodhead did not bring me in."

Coach K also expressed his disappointment over the way that Duke handled the situation. He said, "One thing I wish we would have done differently is to say, 'Those are our kids and we are going to support them because they are still our kids.' That's what I wish we would have done. And I'm not sure we did. I don't think we did a good job of that." He also stated that "there have been fraternity parties and kegs for years. Kids misbehaved in college forty years ago and they are still misbehaving . . . the kids are not running wilder here any more than in any other place."

His concern was that Duke's image was hurt because of the way the kids were treated. "People feel we left the kids unsupported." It struck me that Coach K used the word "we." He tried to come to the aid of Brodhead on the issue and was rejected. He could have easily pointed the finger at Brodhead or used the word "he" or "they," but he didn't. He is a great leader and a team player even when slighted. When he did make a public statement in June of 2006 about the lacrosse situation, he spoke on behalf of the boys, and he did say that they are our kids and we are going to support them. When I read about his statement at that time, I thought that it was the first true voice of reason that I had heard on behalf of the school, and I wished that others would follow that lead. It is amazing to me that Brodhead did not call for Coach K's help when this story broke in the media. Mike Krzyzewski is not only the most recognizable figure at Duke, he has an unbelievable talent for knowing the right things to say during difficult times. Besides, what better ambassador could Duke have asked for at a time like that?

During the interview, Coach K mentioned his surprise and disappointment at the approximately one hundred Duke professors who had come out publicly against the team. Calling it a "latent hostility" against athletes and sports, he commented that he "thought it was inappropriate."

The show was inspiring and entertaining. It discussed Coach K's life from his childhood with his Polish parents to his acceptance to West Point and his impressive history that led him to Duke. He has been there for approximately twenty-seven years and his incredible record and reputation precede him. But there are some things that many people do not know about him. According to Coach K's website, in 1997, at the University Founders' Day, Coach K was awarded Duke's highest award, the Medal of Honor.

In 2000, Coach K was honored as the first winner of the Verizon Reads with the NABC Literacy Award. In September 2001, he and his wife, Mickie, created the Krzyzewski Family Scholarship Endowment for Duke students from the Carolinas. The $100,000 scholarship, the result of the Krzyzewskis's gift and additional funds from the Duke Endowment of Charlotte, provides assistance to undergraduates from North and South Carolina.

During the fall of 2002, Coach K received an Honorary Alumnus Award from the Duke University Medical Center for his contributions to the Duke Children's Health Center. Coach K and his family have made the center a focal point in their efforts to raise the standard of clinical care for children. In 2003, he launched the K Academy, a summer fantasy camp that assists with a number of basketball projects. "The Center's mission is to build a better future for the children and families in our community by creating an environment that fosters the development of life skills that are fundamental to reaching one's highest potential. The longer term goal is to identify, develop and nurture the future leaders of the community in a way that prepares them to achieve excellence in their field of choice, act as role models and mentors, and encourages them to engage in and lead change in their communities."

Coach K's site also says that university students play an important role in his life. He often buys pizza for those students who live in "Krzyzewskiville," a tent community erected each season outside of Cameron Indoor Stadium that enables students to get in line early for tickets to the home basketball games. Coach K also treats them to pre-game strategy plans inside of Cameron. He and his team have a unique relationship with the students; that relationship, he feels, is one of the things that makes Duke so special. The site says that those students, also known as the "Cameron Crazies," are regarded as some of the best fans in all of sports. The Cameron Crazies have created an atmosphere for Duke basketball games that has made Cameron Indoor Stadium one of the most famous and exciting venues in all of sports.

Coach K has also led the fund-raising efforts for and is Chair of the Board of Directors of the Emily Krzyzewski Family Life Center, a community center that opened in February 2006 and was named in honor of his mother.

This is the side of coaching and athletics that people rarely have the opportunity to see. Men like Coach K not only give their lives to their teams, but they do so much for many others. These are the men who often have the biggest impact on the lives of so many young people, not just with respect to sports, but in developing athletes in ways that make each of them strive to be better people.

As you may have noticed from the last few pages of this book, I am a big Coach K fan. That is why I made it a point to watch the *Costas* show that featured a segment about him. The show included a part that revealed a little bit more about the man behind the reputation and coaching achievements, which I found very inspiring. There was a touching moment on the show. It was when Coach K's daughter talked about what it was like attending school the day after her father's Duke team had lost a basketball game against North Carolina, its biggest rival. The kids verbally harassed her and made fun of her all day because of the Duke loss. It became so intolerable for her that she called him and asked him to come and get her out of there. His response was, "You're not leaving school, but I'll bring you a Duke sweatshirt." She said that as soon as she heard that, she thought, "I got it. I got it." What a great way to respond to any challenge—with courage, a sense of pride, and strong determination. I only hope that Evans, Finnerty, and Seligmann had their televisions on when Coach K was talking.

Fortunately, these extraordinary young men are still intact, in spite of all that has happened to them and what occurred around them at Duke. In fact, they have almost surely grown stronger from this terrible experience. And that came across loud and clear as they each spoke, surrounded by their families, their attorneys, and their teammates on the day that the charges were dropped. Evans described the experience of the past "395 days" by saying that the team had "gone to hell and back." He expressed his support for Finnerty and Seligmann, explaining that their ordeal was different than his in that they were ripped out of school while he had already graduated and reached a point in his life where he could take some time off. He also sent out a message to universities across the country about Finnerty and Seligmann asking that they offer the boys their "support and aid." In a show of admiration for the lacrosse team, he said, "If you want to know what character is, walk around your campus and see signs with your picture on it equating you to Hitler when you've done nothing wrong. That is character to sit there and take that as the young men of the Duke University Lacrosse team did." And he talked about the lack of controls on the grand jury proceedings in North Carolina, stressing that the issue is one that should be addressed. In closing, he commented that he hoped the allegations would not come to define him, and he thanked "the professionalism of the Attorney General's Office for giving [him] back [his] life."

Finnerty expressed his gratitude to his attorneys, his family, and others who had supported him throughout the ordeal. He called the year a "very long and emotional" one and commented that he was comforted knowing that he had the truth on his side. He also mentioned that he is not going to miss all of the media attention that he had experienced over the past year.

Seligmann, after expressing his sadness at the absence of his former attorney, the late J. Kirk Osborn, on "this very emotional day," described the experience as "a dark cloud of injustice that hung above our heads." He thanked his family for keeping him "focused" and "bolstering [his] spirit throughout this agonizing journey" and said he was "inspired by the courage and strength" of his parents and siblings who provided him with "love, guidance and unquestionable faith" in his innocence. He also directed his criticism to those who spoke out against the boys with "hurtful words" and "outrageous lies," after which he poignantly quoted Abraham Lincoln, saying that "Truth is the best vindication against slander."

Now we see what has truly carried the Duke Three and their teammates through one of the most tumultuous times that they will hopefully ever have to endure.

The courage, sense of pride, and strong determination that resonated from Coach K's words on the *Costas* show were in full display on April 11, not only in the Duke Three's words, but by the show of support that came from the lacrosse team members as they headed to the press conference.

From time to time, I, along with other former Duke athletes and supporters, receive e-mails from Art Chase, Duke University's Sports Information Director, which provide updates or interesting information on Duke athletics. Mr. Chase sent us an interesting e-mail on Thursday, April 12, 2007, describing his experience from the previous day when Roy Cooper dropped the charges against the boys. These were his words:

At 2:30 p.m., the men's and women's lacrosse teams boarded two buses outside the Murray Building to drive to Raleigh and attend the press conference held by the defense lawyers and three accused young men. One bus housed the women's team—all thirty-one members plus coaches and support staff—while the second bus was filled with thirty-four players (four went on their own and three had academic commitments), two assistant coaches, support staff and Sue Pressler, the wife of former head coach Mike Pressler.

We tuned the radio to listen to the press conference of the Attorney General. As Roy Cooper dismissed the charges, I watched and listened to the players. There was no jubilation, no cheering and no excitement. Rather, it was silent. The look on their faces was one of relief. These young men understood that their former teammates had been wrongfully accused, but they took no satisfaction in the fact that Cooper's remarks cast a poor light on District Attorney Mike Nifong.

After the defense lawyers' press conference, the current players greeted their former teammates behind a curtain away from the masses of media. Handshakes were non-existent—it was a time for bear hugs. The thirty-three current members of the Duke team that were at one time suspects in this case all felt that it could have been "me" enduring the process over the past year that David Evans, Reade Seligmann and Collin Finnerty and their families went through. Their support for one another throughout the past year has been nothing short of amazing.

These boys can certainly continue to walk through their lives with their heads held high because they have done nothing wrong and the State of North Carolina has finally vindicated them. They can also take great pride for the strength, courage, and dignity with which they have conducted themselves while they endured this outrageous injustice.

Like Reade Seligmann, I hope that Colin Finnerty and David Evans can also find encouragement and comfort from Rudyard Kipling's inspirational poem mentioned earlier, the one that Seligmann said is the only thing that has helped him sleep at times during the past year. It is called "If," and it is filled with words of wisdom that could provide great comfort to any of us when facing difficult circumstances:

> If you can keep your head when all about you
> Are losing theirs and blaming it on you;
> If you can trust yourself when all men doubt you,
> But make allowance for their doubting too;
> If you can wait and not be tired by waiting,
> Or, being lied about, don't deal in lies,
> Or, being hated, don't give way to hating,
> And yet don't look too good, nor talk too wise;
>
> If you can dream—and not make dreams your master;
> If you can think—and not make thoughts your aim;
> If you can meet with triumph and disaster
> And treat those two imposters just the same;
> If you can bear to hear the truth you've spoken
> Twisted by knaves to make a trap for fools,
> Or watch the things you gave your life to broken,
> And stoop and build 'em up with wornout tools;
>
> If you can make one heap of all your winnings
> And risk it on one turn of pitch-and-toss,
> And lose, and start again at your beginnings

And never breath a word about your loss;
If you can force your heart and nerve and sinew
To serve your turn long after they are gone,
And so hold on when there is nothing in you
Except the Will which says to them: "Hold on";

If you can talk with crowds and keep your virtue,
Or walk with kings—nor lose the common touch;
If neither foes nor loving friends can hurt you;
If all men count with you, but none too much;
If you can fill the unforgiving minute
With sixty seconds' worth of distance run—
Yours is the Earth and everything that's in it,
And—which is more—you'll be a Man my son!

I leave you with one thought. I do not believe that things happen by chance; everything happens for a reason. To paraphrase scripture, God makes us experience trials and difficult challenges in order to afford us the opportunity to grow and mature. In the words of the man affectionately known to Dukies as Coach K: "I believe God gave us crises for some reason—and it certainly wasn't for us to say that everything about them is bad. A crisis can be a momentous time for a team to grow—if a leader handles it properly."

EPILOGUE

"Justice denied anywhere diminishes justice everywhere."
—Martin Luther King, Jr.

The greatness of our country will always balance on the fulcrum of incidents like the one you have just read about. And as you have discovered, much of what happened frames the darkness that seems to lurk in the hearts of some who would prefer to choose expediency or self-interest over righteousness.

But, in spite of the rush to injustice, there is some redemption found in this incident, and I believe that good can come out of it. The boys will be stronger and more mature I cannot envision a challenge that they won't be prepared for having survived this ordeal.

Duke can use this opportunity to take a closer look at its leaders, to do a better job of reminding its students how to steer clear of potential nightmares, and to avoid jumping to unfortunate conclusions when allegations are leveled.

Our legal justice system must purge itself of individuals in positions of authority who commit outrageous acts of misconduct, and severely punish those people who commit these acts.

Finally, I believe that we all can learn a good lesson about not being too quick to judge others, to give others the benefit of the doubt, and to not be blinded by race or prejudice of any kind. God has created us different, wonderfully unique. That is a good thing. You and I should never treat others with prejudice for any reason. We should never allow ourselves the luxury of judging others harshly.

EPILOGUE

This story has shed a penetrating light on the consequences of such foolishness. Let it be a lesson to us all.

"America is great because she is good. If America ceases to be good, America will cease to be great."

—ALEXIS DE TOCQUEVILLE

EKSTRAND TIMELINE

DATE: March 13, 2006–March 14, 2006

*Prior to the party at some point, Crystal had a "function" at a hotel room where she performed using a "small vibrator."

Around 11 a.m.
> —Team Run & Lift. Team had returned from San Diego trip prior day.

9:05 p.m.
> —Crystal receives a call. (No Call ID, 2 minutes)

9:32 p.m.
> —Crystal receives a call. (919-XXX-XXXX, 2 minutes)

9:46 p.m.
> —Crystal receives a call. (919-XXX-XXXX, 1 minute)

11:00 p.m.
> —The time the girls were scheduled to arrive to dance for 2 hours ($800 paid up front).

11:02:36 p.m.
> —Picture: boys hanging out.

11:11 p.m.
> —Crystal receives short phone call. (No Call ID, 1 minute)

11:22 p.m.

—Crystal receives a short phone call. (No Call ID, 2 minutes)

11:25 p.m.

—Crystal called her father for 7 minutes. (919-XXX-XXXX, end of call at 11:32 p.m.)

11:33 p.m.

—Crystal receives a call. (No Call ID, 1 minute)

11:36 p.m.

—Crystal receives a call. (No Call ID, 3 minutes. Crystal could not have arrived at the party prior to 11:39 p.m.)

11:50 p.m.–12:00 a.m.

—The girls are seen going over their routine outside by Bissey, they then change and get ready for their dance. Bissey: "Twice that I noticed during this conversation, a man or two different men opened the back door of 610 and spoke to the women, and the more conservatively dressed woman responded both times something to the effect that they would 'be right there,' or 'just give us a minute.'"

12:00 a.m.–12:04 a.m.

—Dance

12:00:12 a.m.

—Picture: Crystal is flat on the ground; face in carpet, Nikki is touching her shoulder with her right hand. Boys are sort of smiling, sort of incredulous. Crystal's right shoe is already off (it is pictured on the floor right behind her).

12:00:21 a.m.

—Picture: Crystal on hands and knees, Nikki straddling her standing up; most boys are beginning to look away from them; one is pictured keying in a text message on his phone; one is looking down at his feet; one of the girls is very close to one of the boys, who is leaning away just holding his cup. ZOOM IN ON RIGHT HEEL (small laceration, later referred to in SANE report: she came to the party with the wounds later referenced to by Nifong as evidence she was raped).

12:00:29 a.m.

—Picture: (CALIBRATION SHOT—WATCH WORN BY PERSON IN PICTURE SHOWS TIME THAT IS CONSISTENT WITH TIMESTAMP IN METADATA.) Crystal is now lying on back. Left thumb nail is seen not painted and without press-on nail affixed at all. Police and Nifong have claimed her fingernails came off in struggle. Reade's face borders on fright (leaning away from them). NIKKI IS CLEARLY LAUGHING/SMILING.

12:00:40 a.m.

—Picture: pseudo oral stimulation; boys looking away and texting. ZOOM IN ON RIGHT KNEE (scratch on knee, later referred to in SANE report and claimed by Nifong to be evidence of rape/struggle; that Crystal came to 610 with it).

12:02:16 a.m.

—Picture: Crystal hovering over Nikki, who is on her back; her pinky fingernail is not polished nor is press-on affixed. Boy shown with "thumbs down." Boy holding cup over girls. NIKKI IS CLEARLY LAUGHING/SMILING; the boys are now clearly disinterested in the dance.

12:02:46 a.m.

—Picture: Girls are still in the room. Sometime after 12:02:16 a.m., non-threatening exchange about broomstick occurs. Boy sitting on a stool in the doorway between the living room and "Beirut" room says, "Do you have any toys?" Kim says "no . . ." and the boy says "why don't you use this?" (referring to a broom that was leaning against the wall). Kim in a delayed response says, "that's it . . . (cursing) . . . we are out of here . . . can't talk to us like that . . ."

12:03:57 a.m.

—Picture: girls shown leaving room; everything has been picked up off of the floor (except for Crystal's shoe for right foot), and the girls are exiting the room through the "Beirut" room door.

12:05:37 a.m.

—Reade calls girlfriend.

12:06:13 a.m.

—Reade calls girlfriend.

12:06:51 a.m.

—Reade calls girlfriend.

12:10:03 a.m.

—Reade calls girlfriend.

12:12:05 a.m.

—Reade calls girlfriend.

12:13:21 a.m.

—Reade calls girlfriend.

12:05–12:15 a.m.

—Girls are in house, picking up clothes, boys trying to get them out, and the two girls shut themselves in the bathroom alone for a period of time.

12:14 a.m.

—Reade calls Elmostafa for taxicab. This call is verified on Elmostafa's call log (incoming 973-XXX-XXXX, 1 minute).

12:19 a.m.

—Reade is picked up by taxicab. The cab picks Reade and Rob up at the corner of Watts Street and Urban Avenue (2–4 minute walk).

12:15–12:25 a.m.

—Kim and Crystal leave the house out the back door and Kim gets into her car, Crystal heads around back to go in and "retrieve her shoe." (Jason Bissey Statement)

12:24:12–12:25:23 a.m.

—Reade pictured at ATM.

12:26 a.m.

—Crystal places phone call to Centerfold.

12:30:12 a.m.

—Picture: First picture of Crystal on back stoop; lights are on in kitchen; spotlight is on, Crystal is on the porch, looking down at Dave's dop kit, she also has her purse. She has one shoe on.

12:30:24 a.m.

—Picture: Same general picture, Accuser appears to be unzipping her purse.

12:30:34 a.m.

—Picture: Doormat is visible and in a square position viz. landing and stairs (versus post-fall placement).

12:30:47 a.m.

—Picture: Accuser smiles. She is still looking down into Dave's dop kit and/or her purse. Clothes are fully intact.

12:37:58 a.m.

—Picture: First picture post-fall. Accuser is lying on her side on the stoop; doormat is out of place from its original position.

12:38:18 a.m.

—Picture: Dark view of same picture; door is more open; doormat is visible and the rugs are displaced. Beer can is visible and has not moved (Accuser had apparently cleared that step safely before tripping onto the landing). Once people are aware of Crystal passed out, Kim is asked to please wait while they get her in the car before she leaves.

12:41:32 a.m.

—Picture: (CALIBRATION SHOT—WATCH IS CONSISTENT WITH TIMESTAMP IN METADATA) Accuser is being helped into co-dancer's car. It is clear that Kim had changed because her top is clearly not her dancing garb. We know this is Kim driving because the driver's earrings are identical to the earrings worn by "Nikki" during the dance.

EKSTRAND TIMELINE

12:46 a.m.

—Reade swipes Duke Card into dorm. Reade was dropped off with Rob Wellington between approximately 12:40 a.m. and 12:45 a.m.

12:53:17 a.m.

—911 call by Kim (Disturbance)

—Call take finished 12:54:12 a.m.

—1st Dispatch Officer Stewart (ID *9429*, Unit 212) 12:55:17 a.m.

—2nd Dispatch Sgt. Shelton (ID *4971*, Unit 200) 12:55:25 a.m.

12:55:25 a.m.

—1st Police vehicle Sgt. Shelton (ID *4971*, Unit 200) arrives at 610 Buchanan, 1:06:59 a.m.—cleared

12:56:43 a.m.

—2nd Police vehicle (ID *9429*, Unit 212) arrives at 610 Buchanan, 1:06:00 a.m.—cleared

12:58:10 a.m.

—"I'm at the alley about a half block down from where you are."

12:58:19 a.m.

—"I'm standing right here on the sidewalk actually on Buchanan . . . at uh 610 right now."

12:58:28 a.m.

—"I walked up there and walked down the back to see (a little inaudible) but they'd already left."

12:58:43 a.m.

—"610 uh Buchanan but there's nobody here . . . they've all already left."

12:58:52 a.m.

—"I have two of the units out with me . . . we're gonna do a little knock and talk . . . see who is home."

1:00 a.m.

—Bissey estimates that he sees "the car he had seen parked in front of 610 headed north on Buchanan towards Markham." This suggests that Bissey's timeline is roughly 5 minutes fast because Kim drives off for good only after she completes her 911 call to report a racial slur (at 12:53:17 a.m.). "Most of the men were walking toward Duke's East Campus, but some proceeded to the West toward Watts St. Before the car was parked in front of 610 sped off, I distinctly heard one young man's voice who was walking toward East Campus. He yelled at the car that was driving off, 'Hey bitch, thank your grandpa for my nice cotton shirt.'

1:00–1:30 a.m.

—Some time within this 1/2 hour Jarriel Johnson receives a call from Tammy who asks him if he was Crystal's driver that night. He responds, "No." Tammy hangs up. (Jarriel Johnson's statement, 4/6/06) He did not hear from Crystal until Thursday, March 16, 2006.

1:22:29 a.m.

—911 call by Kroger Security Officer (Entered nature— 1:22:52 intoxicated person, entered remarks 1:23:41 entered caller name—1:23:41 Kim)

—Call take finished 1:23:53 a.m.

—1st Dispatch Officer Barfield (ID *7745*, Unit 222)

1:27:30 a.m.

—2nd Dispatch Sgt. Shelton (ID *4971*, Unit 200)

1:32:22 a.m.

—1st Police vehicle Sgt. Shelton (ID *4971*, Unit 200) arrives at Kroger, 1:49:02 a.m.—cleared

1:33:55 a.m.

—Officer Barfield brings Crystal to Durham Access and is followed by Officer Stewart. As they are leaving, Barfield says, "She's, she's breathing appears to be fine. She's not in distress. She's just passed out drunk."

1:37:27 a.m.

—2nd Police vehicle Officer Barfield (ID *7745*, Unit 222) arrives at Kroger, 4:54:07 a.m.—cleared

1:49:12 a.m.

—To: Durham Access/24032 BM (Transport), Officer Barfield (ID *7745*, Unit 222), arrived 1:55:41 a.m. 24036 EDM

1:55 a.m.

—Approximate arrival at Durham ACCESS.

Once there, she said her name was "Honey" and she said that "she did not want to go to jail." She was led into a treatment room where she was interviewed by a registered nurse. To that nurse, the woman's thoughts appeared disorganized and not logical. The nurse worked with her over the course of several minutes and "because it was evident that [she] may not be capable of maintaining her lucid thinking I began (unlike the format of other interviews) to zero in with questions . . . I simply asked her if she had been raped and she began to retreat and guard herself as she nodded yes." She further related that "the woman from Angela's had taken her money and insisted that she get out of the car."

2:12:8 a.m.

—"Alright um yeah call and see if you can't get somebody close to Charles Street to ride by there and check on the youngens."

2:31:44 a.m.

—To: Duke ER/24036 BM (Transport), Officer Barfield (ID *7745*, Unit 222)—arrived 2:40:28 a.m. 24040 EDM

2:37:07 a.m.

—"She's uh on the way to Duke now . . . and they gonna get a SANE nurse, fill out the report and uh I'll let you know where we are at that point." Another Officer responds, "Alright, if that's what you all gonna do." First Officer responds back "That's your job (big daddy/big thing?)"

2:39:03 a.m.

—"The woman we talked to at the Kroger knew her?" Another Officer responds, "quite possibly . . . worked together."

2:39:04 a.m.

—Officer Sutton (ID *8819*, Unit 223) Dispatched, Arrived

2:40:28 a.m.

—Officer Barfield (ID *7745*, Unit 222) and Transport arrive at 24040 EDM

2:42 a.m.

—Noted arrival time by law enforcement on hospital records.

2:44:35 a.m.—

6:14:30 a.m.—cleared

2:45:47 a.m.

—Location Change by Officer Sutton (ID *8819*, Unit 223)—Duke Medical Center

2:50:22 a.m.

—Changed Nature (Intoxicated Person—RAPE)

3:08 a.m.

—Operations Report Duke University Police Department by Christopher H. Day (116). In the report, Day says that the female claimed that "she was raped by approximately 20 males at 610 N. Buchanan Street." Day reports that "PO Mazurek contacted Lt. Best in reference to the victim. Lt. Best stayed at the Emergency Department to gather information from the victim with the Durham Police. PO Eason, PO Robertson, and I went to 610 N. Buchanan Street to follow up and see if we could make contact with the occupants of the house . . . The victim changed her story several times, and eventually Durham Police stated that charges would not exceed misdemeanor simple assault against the occupants of 610 N. Buchanan. There were no charges filed by Duke Police Officers. No suspects have been identified at this time."

3:13:55 a.m.

—Officer Stewart (ID *9429*, Unit 212) responded to disturbance at 610 dispatched and arrived. 3:35:46 a.m.—cleared

3:50 a.m.

—Investigator B. S. Jones (ID *7153*) responded to Duke ER in reference to a sexual assault call.

4:54:07 a.m.

—Officer Barfield (ID *7745*, Unit 222)—cleared

6:14:30 a.m.

—Officer Sutton (ID *8819*, Unit 223)—cleared

7:30 a.m.

—Official report of the Duke Police Department was submitted and reviewed by Duke Police Director Robert Dean.

1:37 p.m.

—Crystal Mangum is discharged from Duke University Hospital.

1:40 p.m.

—Investigator Jones awoke to find a voicemail from Ms. Mangum. Jones called Ms. Mangum back and left her a message that Sergeant Gottlieb would be handling her case from this point on and gave her his contact information.

INDEX

INDEX

INDEX

INDEX

witness statements, 22, 65, 113
Wolf, Naomi, 82–83
Wolfe, Tom, 44
Wood, Peter, 217
WRAL-TV, 65, 75, 80

Y
Yale Daily News, 83
Yale University, 81–82

Z
Zash, Matt, 9, 12, 28, 31, 67